A Biblical Merry-Go-Round

AND OTHER ESSAYS

By

Arthur Babb

Edited, Annotated and with an Introduction by
STEVEN R. BUTLER

THE FREETHOUGHT PRESS OF TEXAS

Richardson, Texas

FOR ARTHUR.

The most helpful man and friend I never met.

FIRST EDITION

Printed in the United States of America

www.freethoughtpressoftexas.com

CONTENTS

INTRODUCTION

Arthur Babb, my first cousin three times removed
and a man I unfortunately never met, was neither rich nor
famous, nor was he known outside his own small circle of
family, friends, and co-workers. Born in a rustic log cabin
at Fairfield, Texas on October 31, 1865, he grew up in a
succession of rural communities where his total time in
school came to less than one year. Yet despite this
educational handicap, Arthur managed to transcend his
humble beginnings. Starting out as a farmer, he went on to
work as a railroad carpenter, architect, building contractor,
and finally, during his old age, a bookbinder. Endowed
with natural intelligence and inquisitiveness, Arthur also
managed to acquire knowledge and make up for his lack of
formal schooling by becoming a voracious reader of
books, magazines, and newspapers. His seemingly
inherent ability to think critically—to investigate, analyze
and draw conclusions from his reading, served him well.
At some point he pondered the question of whether or not
the God of the Bible actually existed. After careful
consideration he concluded that the answer was "no."

In 1925, when he was nearly sixty years old,
Arthur began writing his *Life Book*, a memoir in which he
recollected his early years growing up and coming of age
in rural nineteenth century Texas. Remembering the
people who were near and dear to him throughout this
period of his life, Arthur recalled that his mother, Lucy
Ann Babb, was "considerably better" educated "than the
average person of her time." Moreover, he wrote, "She
was well-versed in Astronomy and Geology, and other

courses of study in this time."[1] In light of evidence that Arthur eventually became equally "well versed" in such topics, we may conclude that his mother had a significant influence on her young son's intellectual development.

Arthur also recollected that although his mother possessed a better-than-average knowledge of natural science, she was also "religiously-inclined," having been raised "under the influence of the Presbyterian faith," although she was "broad of views" and "held to no particular creed, regarding them as a matter which placed more confidence in your conduct than in your faith." Lucy Ann's well-worn, dog-eared, leather-bound Holy Bible, which has survived to the present day, provides tangible evidence of her religious faith, which included belief "in miracles, the immaculate conception of Jesus, etc." But Arthur was different, as he remembered:

> I know now, more than then, how I must have annoyed her with my skepticism, with which she tried hard to be patient, and I tried hard to restrain. She would say, *"I do not understand why the boy asks such questions!"* And the boy did not understand, but I do now. It was that inquisitive faculty that makes men seek for truth, beginning to assert itself.[2]

Although Arthur was admittedly doubtful as a boy, it appears that he was not entirely lacking in religious faith either. In one of his stories about his childhood, he recollected that when meteor showers and an eclipse of the sun led people in his community to worry that the end of the world was coming—and this not long after he had acquired his first horse—he decided "to take my troubles to the Lord," recalling in his *Life Book*:

---

[1] Steven R. Butler, *Tales of Northeast Texas: The Life Book & Sketches of Arthur Babb* (Richardson, Texas: Poor Scholar Publications, 1998), 27-8.
[2] Butler, *Tales of Northeast Texas*, 28.

I retired to the peach orchard and took a position as I thought most pleasing to his sight and asked God most earnestly to reconsider this rash act that I had heard he was contemplating at this most important time. I called his attention to the fact, as he well knew, that I had worked so long and patiently to get my pony to where I could ride her. To be robbed of this pleasure was too much!

And the Lord, as he did when speaking with Moses *(Ex 22 - 14)*, *"repented of the evil that he had intended to do,"* and my prayer was answered.[3]

Arthur concluded this story by remarking (almost certainly tongue-in-cheek): "Perhaps I have been of some service to the world after all."[4]

Precisely when Arthur adopted the views he propounds in this book—namely that all religions are manmade and not only is there no "God" but also no afterlife and no soul—is unknown. Perhaps, as often happens, his abandonment of faith in favor of reason was a gradual process that began in young adulthood and reached completion in mid-life.

In 1926, when he was not quite sixty-one-years old, the Texas and Pacific Railway sent Arthur to Plaquemine and Natchitoches, Louisiana to supervise the building of railroad depots. During the several months he was away from home he kept a journal or *Sketchbook* in which his earliest known critical references to religion can be found.

At Plaquemine, for instance, Arthur remarked that the Cajuns he encountered were hospitable people but "very religious, strongly flavored with superstition." Some of their practices, he wrote, reminded him "of primitive man building bonfires and shooting arrows at the storm clouds." Prompted by these observations, he wondered:

---

[3] Butler, *Tales of Northeast Texas*, 38.
[4] Ibid.

"How long will it be before reason will sufficiently develop in the mind of mankind to direct our actions intelligently?"[5]

When Arthur visited the tiny one-room Palo Alto Chapel at Iberville, reportedly the smallest church in the world, he remarked that there were similar shrines in Asia paying homage to Buddha and pondered: "Who is right? I wonder."[6] At Carville, Louisiana he visited a Leper Colony, where he contrasted Jesus, who reportedly performed a miracle by curing a single leper, with the staff of the institution where no fewer than twenty-eight lepers had been cured by modern medicine. He concluded this section by quoting the "Great Agnostic," Robert G. Ingersoll: "The hand that helps is far better than the lips that pray."[7]

After Arthur retired he had much more time for reading and to thoroughly acquaint himself with the works of scientists and thinkers such as Charles Darwin and Thomas Huxley—men who advanced a scientific and natural, as opposed to a supernatural explanation for the existence of the world and everything in it, including human beings. Residing for a time within walking distance of Southern Methodist University, Arthur informally improved his meager education by frequenting the school's library. He also knew some of the professors who taught at SMU—men and women who generously gave him their time and the benefit of their knowledge. To earn money he became a bookbinder, which also provided him the opportunity to peruse the contents of the various books he was given to repair while they were in his possession. Arthur was also a regular reader of newspapers (usually the *Dallas Morning News* and/or the *Dallas Journal*) as well as magazines (his favorites seem to have been the

[5] Neil Cameron, ed., *My Sketchbook by Arthur Babb* (Natchitoches, Louisiana: Northwestern State University Press, 1996), 10-11.
[6] Ibid., 33-4.
[7] Ibid., 39.

Readers Digest, Coronet, National Geographic, and *LIFE*). Additionally, Arthur had his own meticulously inventoried personal library, which consisted largely of major works by not only Darwin and Huxley but also Voltaire, Victor Hugo, H. G. Wells, Herbert Spencer, Charles A. Beard, Henry David Thoreau, J. Frank Dobie, and Thomas Paine. Arthur's library also included a number of volumes about the world's religions, which he almost certainly consulted when writing the first two parts of this book. From all appearances, the result of all this independent study was to reinforce conclusions Arthur had already arrived at earlier by himself.

It is difficult to know, owing to the absence of either term in his writing, whether Arthur considered himself an "atheist" (someone who is certain there is no god) or an "agnostic" (someone who sees no evidence of a supreme being but is willing to concede the possibility even though it seems unlikely). Unfortunately, the only label he ever gave himself was "heretic." It should be pointed out, however, that much of Arthur's writing, whether on religion or other topics, often concludes with these inquisitive words: *"Who knows, I wonder?"* For this reason, it seems more likely that he would have preferred the term "agnostic," which was coined by Thomas Huxley (known in his time as "Darwin's Bulldog") and adopted by such well-known skeptics as Robert Ingersoll, with whose works Arthur was well-acquainted.

⁂

This work is divided into three parts. The first, which in its original form consists of fifty-one typed, double-spaced pages, was written in 1944, apparently during the latter part of the year, when the author was seventy-nine years old and the end of the Second World War was rapidly approaching. At the time he wrote it, Arthur was living in a private convalescent home in East

Dallas, where he was one of five male patients.[8] It is remarkable that he somehow managed to compose this lengthy essay with only one good eye (the other was then nearly blinded by a cataract, which was later successfully removed). The second part consisted of seventeen pages (likewise typed and double-spaced). Based on Arthur's references to then-current events, it was apparently composed between February and July 1945.

The first part of this work traces the development of religion in general, from the primitive era to modern times. Arthur's obvious intent was to challenge the veracity of various religious writing, beliefs, and claims by drawing attention to the many inconsistencies and contradictions contained in religious texts, particularly the *Bible*, with which Arthur seems to have been reasonably well acquainted (although he doesn't always get his quotes quite right). This section concludes with a list of sixteen gods or religious figures in history whose life stories bear a remarkable resemblance to that of Jesus Christ.

Some of the main points of Part One are as follows:

- All religions are manmade (see page 5, "and God was made in man's own image").
- There is an abnormal obsession with blood and sacrifice in religion.
- Religion is mythological in nature and based on fear.
- All the major religions of the world can be traced back to one source, the Hindu Vedas.

---

[8] Although Arthur did not identify the home by name or address in writing, based on his description of the place and an interview I conducted with his granddaughter in 2013, I believe that it was probably the now non-existent Garrett Park Convalescent Home, located at 1413 N. Garrett Avenue, directly across the street from Garrett Park.

- Jesus Christ was the not the first "Savior of the World." There were no fewer than sixteen others before him.
- As God is portrayed in the *Bible*, he is neither loving nor merciful.
- People often say they believe things about their religion that they don't really believe, for fear of being ostracized.
- Many *Bible* stores are contradictory or simply make no sense.
- Most religious claims are simply not possible "to say nothing of true or reasonable."
- No religion can stand up to critical examination.
- Organized religion is similar to the organization of armies.
- During the Dark Ages, church members were deliberately kept in ignorance.
- Christian ministers use fear of Hell to persuade people to accept Jesus as their savior.

Arthur also uses Part One to ask some pointed questions and to make some telling remarks:

- If the Biblical account of creation is true, then why isn't it taught in school?[9]

---

[9] Although Arthur lived many decades before the present-day controversy surrounding the proposed teaching of so-called "Intelligent Design" in school, he surely must have remembered the "Scopes Monkey Trial" of 1925, which resulted from the State of Tennessee banning the teaching of Darwin's Theory of Evolution in public schools. I am very surprised that he did not mention it.

- If God can see and know everything, why did he have so much trouble finding Adam when he was hiding in the Garden of Eden?
- God said that Adam and Eve would die if they ate from the Tree of Knowledge but they did not.
- Judas was framed; he ought not to be looked down upon for carrying out his assigned role in the crucifixion.
- The story of Noah and the Flood cannot be true because scientists tell us that every drop of water that ever was is still here and there is not enough to inundate the entire surface of the earth.
- If all prayers are answered, then why do we need hospitals?
- It wasn't prayers that made D-Day successful; it was the determination and bravery of our soldiers.
- The story of Moses on Mount Sinai, talking to God in the form of a burning bush, is no less incredible than Joseph Smith's story about the founding of the Mormon Church.

Some of Arthur's comments in this first section were, at least to me, laugh-out-loud funny. I found his story about challenging some other old folks to a prayer test, in which he offered to play the part of "guinea pig," particularly amusing.

The second part of this book, written in the early part of 1945,[10] consists largely of a critique of the Christian religion in particular and explores the question of whether or not human beings possess a soul. Here are

---

[10] We can be certain of the year since Arthur mentions that he has just read an article, "The Mystery of the Stone Towers," which appeared in the March 1945 issue of the *Reader's Digest* magazine.

some of what I think are the best of Arthur's conclusions from this section:

- "Either it [a religious holy book] means just what it says, or it doesn't mean anything."
- "If I accept a thing upon which I can base a belief, it must have supporting evidence."
- "If faith means acceptance of any mythical concept without evidence of scientific support...then we would be better off without it"
- "Faith has never advanced civilization. It may console, but it does not advance. It is science and invention that put us ahead."

The third and final section of this book consists of three short sketches. Apart from being critical of religion, they are unrelated to Parts One and Two. Two of these works—"God in the Prize Ring" and "A Criminal and His Victim"—predate Parts One and Two by nearly twenty years. Both were hand-printed with pencil in 1927 and then afterward bound into the author's collection of miscellaneous material that he titled *This and That*. The third, also printed in pencil but separately bound in a paper-covered pamphlet, is a critical review of an article about science and religion that Arthur read in the December 1946 issue of the *Reader's Digest*.

⁓⊱⊰⁓

In the second part of this book there is a place where the reader can almost see Arthur leaning back in his chair and sighing as he writes, "I wish I had a friend, a thinker, to talk a few subjects over with." Unfortunately, by the time he began writing down his thoughts on reason and religion, the "Golden Age of Freethought" in America was over. During that era, which began shortly after

Arthur was born and lasted until the First World War, people who openly called themselves "freethinkers" formed "liberal leagues" where they could socialize with other non-believers. Freethought publications such as *The Truth Seeker*, the *Index*, and the *Blue Grass Blade* flourished. There was even a National Liberal League, of which the "Great Agnostic," Robert Green Ingersoll, was president.

From 1918 through 1991, most Americans tended to associate atheism with Soviet-style Communism. Even though most if not all American atheists and agnostics were loyal citizens, few of their fellow Americans were either willing or able to make the distinction. Consequently, to openly admit that you did not believe in God or even just had some doubts was to commit social suicide. You could lose your family, your friends, or your job, or all three. In a country where conformity was prized above all else, independent thinkers were pariahs. Throughout this period, only a handful of courageous individuals, such as Joseph Lewis, President of the Freethinkers of America, and Madalyn Murry O'Hair, founder of American Atheists, were willing to openly challenge the status quo. It was therefore prudent for Arthur, during the time he wrote this material, to keep his thoughts to himself or hidden away in his private notebooks.

Although his family was aware that he was not a churchgoer, it appears that he never openly discussed his disbelief with them. The result of his reticence, combined with the fact that he left no will or final instructions, was that his funeral, over which a Methodist minister presided, was replete with all the usual religious ceremony that precedes a so-called "Christian burial." A typewritten description of the service even states that "one of Mr. Babb's favorite scriptures was the Twenty-third Psalm," which is incredibly hard to believe. Unless he underwent a reverse conversion during the last few years of his life of which I have no knowledge, I think he would have been displeased if he could have known what sort of send-off his family arranged for him. Or perhaps he simply did not care, knowing that it was all meaningless anyway. As Arthur would have said: *"Who knows, I wonder?"*

Thankfully, things are different today, which leads me to wonder, if it was possible to go back in time and bring him to the early twenty-first century, what would Arthur make of the present-day contest between religious belief and rational thought? What he would make of the so-called "New Atheists," such as Richard Dawkins, Daniel Dennett, Sam Harris, and the late Christopher Hitchens, all of whom advance many of the same arguments that Arthur was making more than seventy years ago? I do not doubt that he would cheer them on.

I wonder too how Arthur felt about the separation of church and state, a topic about which he says very little in this work. Perhaps that is due to the fact that during his lifetime, the United States was a much less culturally and religiously diverse place than it is today and also because it was not until a few years after he died that Congress put "In God We Trust" on U.S. currency and "under God" in the Pledge of Allegiance. Consequently, the controversy over such blatant violations of the First Amendment simply did not exist in his lifetime. The attempts of the so-called "Religious Right" to influence public policy and the national security threat posed by militant Islamic fundamentalism likewise came about long after Arthur entered into the eternal oblivion that he called his "Heaven." The State of Israel, the focus of religious discord in the Middle East since 1948, had only recently been established when Arthur died. What, *I wonder*, would he have made of all those things?

I do not know whether Arthur meant for this material to be published or if it was simply a private intellectual exercise. Up to now his writing has been seen only by me and a few other privileged individuals, mostly, if not entirely, family members. I am publishing it for three reasons. First of all, because I share the opinions that

Arthur expressed in it. Secondly, because I think his straightforward, conversational style is worthy of a larger audience. Thirdly, because 2015 marks the 150th anniversary of Arthur's birth and bringing his writing to the attention of the public at this particular time not only makes what I think is a fitting tribute to his memory but also a valuable contribution to the so-called "New Atheist" movement of the twenty-first century.

I have tried to treat this work with a light hand. My editing consists mainly of correcting errors in spelling, grammar, punctuation, and sentence structure. I have also added or replaced a few words when it seemed appropriate. In addition, I added footnotes, principally for the purpose of identifying the source for quotes, whenever Arthur failed to do so. Otherwise, this writing is exactly as it was originally composed by Arthur Babb some seven or more decades ago.

Steven R. Butler
September 17, 2015

Note: Since writing the preceding introduction I have become aware that the scholarship of one of the nineteenth century authors that Arthur cites herein, namely Kersey Graves, has been called into question by Richard Carrier, a modern freethought historian. Even so, I think it is important to point out that whether there were sixteen other so-called "saviors" preceding Jesus Christ, or a smaller number, or even none at all, in no way invalidates the core arguments that Arthur makes in this work.

Steven R. Butler
December 22, 2015

PART ONE

"Religion is conceived of Fear, suckled at the breast of Superstition, and worshipped in the temple of Ignorance."

—Arthur Babb

Thor, der Donnergott.

From Frieda Amerlan's *Götter und Helden der alten Germanen* (Meidinger, 1912).

PAGANISM, PAST and PRESENT
Or Other Gods than Ours

Ancient Egypt has three thousand gods and Greece had just about the same. But few of us would like to acknowledge that those pagan gods of yesteryears were the ancestors of our gods of today, but upon a careful research of history we are forced to grant the same.

If our physical forefathers were traced back to the sub-man, some would hesitate to own him. Darwin got into trouble on this score, and if I follow the subject I can only expect the same, but in less proportion of course, in comparison to the man, but not in importance of the subject.

To arrive at something like an understanding of this subject, to form a basis upon which one would feel safe in venturing an intelligent opinion, we must go back to the fundamental principles of human nature to assign causes, and we must be willing to accept facts or evidence leading to facts, as our research may reveal, regardless of traditional opinion or our own prejudices or partiality. Thos. H. Huxley once said, "I had rather have a painful fact than a pleasant fallacy." And again he said, "I will not compromise with error for mental ease."[11] If you are not of the Huxley quality, I would advise you not to enter the field of research, for that is most assuredly sacred ground.

More than a million years ago primitive man shambled from the forest and looked out upon the forces of nature. He saw the vivid flashes of lightning and heard the deep peal of thunder. The winds lashed the branches of the trees. He was in fright. He retreated to his cave to meditate upon those wonderful forces, so much more

---

[11] It appears that these two quotes are Arthur's slightly flawed recollection of a passage in a book by Elbert Hubbard, who said that Huxley "might never compromise with the error for the sake of mental ease, or accept a belief simply because it was pleasant"; from Elbert Hubbard, *Little Journeys to the Homes of the Great*, volume 12 (New York: Wm. W. Wise & Company, 1916), 318.

mighty than himself, and to assign the causes, and to try to appease their wrath. Doubtless there were some weird speculations. Out of this inborn fear it seems many gods were conceived; beasts, fowls, and reptiles were worshipped. The Druids worshipped trees. We would be safe in saying that religion is a child of fear. Someone has said, "The fear of God is the wisdom of man."[12]

Our language is strewn with pagan gods and goddesses. The names of the days of the week are from pagan mythology without an exception, as well as other words commonly used and passed unnoticed. Destiny from "Destona," god of our destiny.[13] Terminal from Terminus, god of the boundary.[14] Easter is the old Anglo-Saxon goddess of Spring, worshipped about 1100 B.C.[15]

We can readily see from past notes that religion was conceived of fear and in its embryonic form found a ready hotbed in the credulous mind of primitive man. And striving to appease that wonderful power that caused the violence to belch flames and earthquakes to rend the earth, he created himself gods and worshipped them. The path of prehistoric man is marked with his altars for burned offerings and the sacrificial. They stand like milestones that mark the deserted roads of dead civilizations, to be picked up and superseded by temples and cathedrals of another age.

It is interesting to note, throughout religious worship, that man in his attempt to appease his deities resorts to the spilling of blood. Why he should conceive a merciful god to be pleased with such a gruesome sight is

---

[12] I have been unable to locate this quote as Arthur gives it. Perhaps he was thinking of Proverbs 9:10, which reads, "The fear of the Lord is the beginning of wisdom." There are similar verses throughout the Old Testament.

[13] I am not sure where Arthur got this information. I have been unable to verify that any of the ancients had a god or goddess named "Destona."

[14] Arthur got this one right.

[15] He is also correct here.

hard to imagine. In India the sacred bull is placed upon a scaffold and thrust to the heart with a lance, while the penitent sinners march beneath and are sprinkled with the atoning blood; while modern day people sing, "Wash me, cleanse me in the blood that flows from Calvary."

It seems that mankind has imagined a bloodthirsty god.

RELIGION
Man Is Deified

Man was the last thing to be deified; and God was made in man's own image. Plato said, "If a camel should make itself a god, it most assuredly would have four feet and a hump on its back."[16] It was a natural thing in the evolution of thought for civilized man to imagine his god like himself instead of a stone image.

Now ponder with yourself and try to explain the difference between a handmade god and a mind-made god.

ORGANIZED RELIGION

The sacred books of the eastern world were written in Zend and Sanskrit; those of the western world in Greek, Latin, and Hebrew.

The oldest mythology that we have an account of, according to Max Muller[17] and other authorities, is the *Rig-Veda*, and Muller claims it to be the oldest religious creed or precept in the known world, dating back to about 2000 B.C. The *Vedas* occupy the same position in Hindu mythology as the *Pentateuch*[18] does to our own. The *Zend-Avesta* is a canon compiled very much like the *Bible*, and the *Vedas* takes place as a part.

---

[16] I have not been able to find this quote but whoever said it, the comparison makes perfect sense to me.

[17] Muller was a nineteenth century German philologist who did extensive work in comparative religion.

[18] The first five books of the Old Testament *Bible*, which also make up the Jewish *Torah*.

The religious precepts of *Vedas* were taught long before the dawn of written history, being passed from teacher to pupil for many centuries.

It may be that the religious concepts that we entertain today had their birth in the valley of the Ganges.

However, later when hieroglyphics and papyrus were invented, the *Vedas* were recorded and found their way over into Egypt and Persia. Manu takes the place in the *Vedas* that Noah did in the book of Moses during the deluge, after which he becomes the father of all mankind. Brahma made Manu his great lawgiver, thus "the laws of Manu." Now I am getting at what I wanted to call attention to. I do not believe that there is a moral code on earth today that does not contain a fact similar, if not identical, to this old Hindu code; the *Zend-Avesta*, the Hammurabi code, the *Talmud*, the *Bible*, the Koran, and many others too numerous to mention, all having their origin in *Rig-Veda*, dating back possibly to 2500 B.C. How did it happen?

If you take the trouble to follow the footprints of the *Vedas*, I think they will explain for they lead directly to the doorsteps of almost, if not every basic religious concept of civilization, including the *Bible*. Jesus made an attempt to break away and give us a "new deal" and paid for it with his life.

SAVIORS OF THE WORLD

But even so, the story of his [Jesus's] birth and death follows the old pattern of the Hindu myth, the same as Muni and Krishna, who were born on the 25th day of December of a virgin and were crucified. Kersey Graves has made a most astounding collection of Sixteen Saviors of the World, born of virgins and crucified.[19]

I cannot refrain here from quoting one parallel of one, Krishna. He was born at Mathura in India about 1200 B.C. He was said to have been born of a Holy Virgin. He retired to the wilderness to meditate, emerging at thirty-two and was called the Savior of the World. He too promised a "new deal" and annulled the laws of Manu. He abolished the caste system; he had twelve disciples and washed their feet; he had a last supper and a betrayer; he was delivered into the hands of sinful men and crucified between two thieves; he ascended on the third day. A painting of this crucifixion is to be found in the British Museum.[20]

We have for authority such authors as Max Muller, Sir William Jones, Kersey Graves, and others. We further find mention of both *Vedas* and [word missing] by Aristotle and Plutarch some three hundred years B.C.

---

[19] See Kersey Graves, *The World's Sixteen Crucified Saviors; Or, Christianity Before Christ, Containing New, Startling, and Extraordinary Revelations in Religious History, which Disclose the Oriental Origin of All the Doctrines, Principles, Precepts, and Miracles of the Christian New Testament, and Furnishing a Key for Unlocking Many of Its Sacred Mysteries, Besides Comprising the History of 16 Heathen Crucified Gods* (Boston: Colby & Rich, Publishers, 1876).
[20] I have unfortunately been unable to find a copy of this picture.

GOD AS REVEALED IN THE *BIBLE*

Have we a merciful God?

Now I am going to spring something on you that I doubt you have ever heard discussed, though it may have rankled in your mind. I have pondered over it for years. Now don't get excited but stop and think. Can you recall in your reading of the Scripture where God ever performed a kind or generous deed? Honest, I cannot. I am not referring to what you have heard preachers say; they are defense attorneys paid to defend their master; the priesthood of every cult will do the same.

"I am the Lord thy God, and a jealous God, and am visiting iniquities upon those that hate me, but showing mercy unto thousands that love me and keep my commandments."[21] The first promise he kept but if he kept the second the Scriptures give no account of it. I believe he

---

[21] The actual quote, which Arthur nearly got right, is from the *Bible*, Exodus 20:5-6, which reads: "I the LORD thy God am a jealous God, visiting the iniquity of the fathers upon the children unto the third and fourth generation of them that hate me; And shewing mercy unto thousands of them that love me, and keep my commandments."

is said to have put a mark on Cain (the mark put there so that the world would not recognize him as a murderer) but Cain was a criminal; he [God] surely did not do much for Abel, notwithstanding that Abel had kept his commandments and tilled the earth.

I am not recording chapter and verse here. I deem the above quotations too familiar for that to be necessary. However, we will say that it is to be found in the first chapter of Genesis. [22]

After the Lord God had created the heavens and earth, he said, "Let us make man." To whom was he speaking? He then takes a rib from man's side and makes a woman. Such a fantastical fabrication. And I cannot think that my reader, he or she, believes it, if they be of lucid minds. It is interesting to note that this old myth is not taught in any institution of higher learning in the civilized world today. If true, why not teach it? If not, why should we believe something that is not true to be good? Back to my first suggestion, it is FEAR!! (Religion was born of fear, suckled at the breast of superstition, and coddled in the lap of policy.)

There has been a day that this expression would have cost me my life, but I am glad to know these hideous old days are behind us, and we no longer fear the sneaking tread of the Inquisition that haunted the thinker of the Dark Ages.

MERCILESS COMMANDS

We hear such commands as "Have no mercy, spare none, not even the sucklers at the breast."[23] And

---

[22] Arthur almost got it right. See Genesis 4:11-16.

[23] I have been unable to find this precise quote in the *Bible* but perhaps Arthur had this one in mind: "*Show no mercy; have no pity! Kill them all – old and young, girls and women and little children...So they went throughout the city and did as they were told.*" (Ezekiel 9:5-7) Sad to report, the Old Testament is full of similar commands from God to kill people, even innocent children.

again we hear that God stopped the Sun that the battle might continue, but we never hear of him stopping the battle.[24] From all accounts we have, God enjoys a wholesale killing as a Mexican would a bullfight.

And do you remember that when the children jeered at old Elijah, this merciful God called out a She Bear—how it ate them all up, forty of them.[25] Now you tell me you believe that? No, you do not. But why don't you say so? It's "fear."

Next we find ourselves tangled with Pharaoh. He [God] appears to Moses in the burning bush. Moses gets his command to lead the children of Israel out of Egypt and while on the way God met him in an inn and tried to kill him (Exodus 4:24). But how do you suppose that Moses escaped such a venerable foe? That was not a very kind act, and the old man then 80 years old. Then he tells Moses to go to Pharaoh and demand the children of Israel be set free, but God said, "I will harden Pharaoh's heart," which he did repeatedly; and all manner of pestilence was sent to Egypt, even causing all the cattle to die (Exodus 9:19). Looks like to me, this was a frame-up on old Pharaoh all the way round, and an excuse for a tyrannical display.

Read the whole of Exodus and see if you can find anything that reveals a God of mercy.

See in the case of Job, when God got into an argument with Satan, he destroyed the whole of Job's generation, together with his flocks and herds, and afflicted Job in a most unmerciful manner, just to prove to the Devil the faithfulness of one man. He must have had a great regard for Satan's opinion. But how about Job's

---

[24] See, Joshua 10:13.
[25] Arthur confused *Elisha* with *Elijah*: *"From there Elisha went up to Bethel. While he was on his way, some small boys came out of the city and jeered at him. 'Go up baldhead,' they shouted, 'go up baldhead!'— The prophet turned and saw them, and he cursed them in the name of the Lord. Then two she-bears came out of the woods and tore forty two of the children to pieces."* (2 Kings 2:23-24)

family? What did they get out of the deal? And what did God gain? It looks to me like the Devil ushered him and gave him "cards and spades" to start with.[26]

Then we read quotations like this: "Let no man say when he is tempted, I am tempted of God, for God cannot be tempted with evil, neither tempt he any man."[27] Still God was tempted by the Devil into killing a whole generation of people and punishing one of his most faithful servants most horribly.

This frame-up process seems to have its origin in the very beginning, according to tradition. When God created man and woman he placed them in the Garden of Eden, where they were surrounded by all kinds of fruit, which were good to eat, but in the midst of the garden he [God] planted the Tree of Life and the Tree of Knowledge of Good and Evil. And then God commanded the man saying, "Of every tree in the garden thou mayest freely eat. But the Tree of Knowledge of Good and Evil thou shalt not eat of it; for in the very day thou eatest thereof thou shall surely die." (It is interesting to note that Man ate but did not die.)[28]

Why should God not want Man to know good from evil?

We can see from what has already been set forth that according to the Scriptures, God has not dealt very mercifully with humanity. He has threatened and scolded, issued edicts and demanded worship. He has pitted one tribe against the other; "Judea thou shalt march against Nineveh, thou shalt smite him with the edge of the sword, have no mercy, spare none, not the sucklers at the breast, all the women with child shall be ripped up. And they went forth and did battle as the Lord had demanded and came back with two baskets of children's heads, seventy-

---

[26] See almost the entire book of Job.
[27] James 1:13.
[28] See Genesis, chapter 2, of the *Bible* for the entire story.

two altogether."[29] And if you wish more along this line, read the 31st chapter of Numbers. I especially call attention to verses 17 & 18.[30] See if you think that Hitler can stage anything to surpass it![31]

Now I refer to Numbers, chapter 25, verses 8 & 9. There you will see that 24,000 innocent people were killed over a love affair. Then turn to Deuteronomy, chapter 24, verse 16; it plainly states that "fathers shall not be put to death for the children, neither shall the children be put to death for the father." A complete reversal. What are we to believe?

THE DEVIL, HELL, AND DAMNATION

And even preceding these atrocities just related, according to the Scriptures, this just God created a Devil, a spirit opposite in purpose and equal in power to that of himself, and provided him with a Hell and a lake that burns continually, burns with fire and brimstone to receive the souls of those people so ruthlessly slaughtered, as well as other generations to follow. And according to his laws, commands, and edicts, one stands such a spare chance to elude it. With all of human weaknesses and faults, together with the frame-ups one has hardly a chance, for it is written "there is none perfect, no not one!"[32]; and just think this all his own work, for he has said, "All things that are were made by me, and without me there was nothing made that was made." And after all this he repented that he had made man. Debating your chances to win, listen to this for it is Scripture: "Broad is the road and wide is the gate that leadeth to destruction and many there be that go in

---

[29] There are plenty of unspeakable acts of violence commanded by God in the *Bible* but I have been unable to find this particular verse. I wish Arthur had cited some reference for it.

[30] This is Arthur's second reference to this event.

[31] It should be remembered that this essay was written before the magnitude of the Holocaust was known.

[32] This quote, from Romans 3:10, actually reads: "There is no one righteous, not even one."

thereat. But straight is the way and narrow is the path that leadeth to life and few there be that find it."[33] Now what chance do you think you stand if this be true?

THE CRUCIFIXION

This preamble is not so much to place the blame but to exonerate the innocent. So in the case of Judas Iscariot, if I were the foreman of a grand jury and the evidence as revealed in the Scripture was brought before me, I would render a No Bill.

Here I wish to call attention to one phrase in the prayer of Jesus on the Mount of Olives. He said, "O my Father (if it be possible) let this cup pass me."[34] If it be true that "nothing is impossible with God"[35] why the prefix? It seems that he should have known that all things were possible with the Father. And again there comes a puzzling question: Why did Jesus not want to carry out his part of the compact as prophesied and written in the Scripture?

The story of the crucifixion is best told in the 26th chapter of Matthew. Look it up.

Jesus had been called "the man of sorrows" and truly said for if he ever smiled neither sacred nor profane history gives an account of it. He fought, cursed, and cried, but never smiled. Now I hear you saying, "Oh no, no, he didn't fight and curse!" Just wait a minute. Don't you remember the time when he and the Apostles went up to Jerusalem to wait for the end of time and while there he went into the Temple and lashed the merchants with a

---

[33] Matthew 7:13-14. The actual and entire quote is: "Enter ye at the strait gate; for wide is the gate and broad is the way that leadeth to destruction, and many there be which go in thereat. Because strait is the gate and narrow is the way, which leadeth unto life, and few there be that find it."

[34] See Matthew 26:39. Arthur left out one word, "from," ("let this cup pass *from* me") but the meaning is essentially unchanged.

[35] Luke 1:37.

piece of rope?[36] And once, when he and the Disciples were walking across country they saw some fig trees on the hill and Jesus suggested that they go thither and get some figs and one of the party protested, "No Master, it is not the season for figs." But he [Jesus] insisted that they go and when they got to the trees there were no figs and he [Jesus] cursed the trees and they wilted and died.[37]

Now we come to the saddest thing of all in the Scripture. Jesus' prayer was not answered; the cup did not pass him and he died a disappointed man. His last words on the cross were, "My God, my God, why hast thou forsaken me?"[38] Then his head drooped forward and he said in a low voice, "It is finished."[39]

But the strangest thing in all the Scripture is that God should descend to earth and beget a child by a Jewish girl and decree that he should be killed as a means to save the world from sin and then it didn't do it.

But "oh boy!" suppose old Adam had got hold of that Tree of Life, wouldn't we have been sitting pretty? But no such good luck. When God came down on his first tour of inspection he caught Adam in the act and drove him from the garden and pronounced a curse upon both him and Eve, together with the snake, notwithstanding that Eve was not present when the command was given or was she even created at the time. And the decree was such that all posterity should inherit the curse. Is that just? And in another place I read, "No man shall be condemned for another's deeds."[40] Did God know that man would transgress when he gave the command? And what would

---

[36] John 2:13-16.
[37] Arthur's account is essentially the same as found in the *Bible*, Mark 11:12-25, except that Jesus only cursed one fig tree, not multiple trees, but the point he [Arthur] was trying to make is still valid.
[38] Matthew 26:46.
[39] John 19:30.
[40] I think the *Bible* verse that Arthur may have had in mind here was Ezekiel 18:20, which reads in part, "The son shall not bear the iniquity of the father; neither shall the father bear the iniquity of the son."

man's station in life have been had he obeyed the command? Would we have all been morons?

"The Pitchers We, whose Maker makes them ill,
Shall He torment them if they chance to spill?"[41]

CREATION

It is amusing to note when God came down for the inspection that Adam hid among the trees and God couldn't find him. But not a sparrow falls without his observation and even the hairs of your head are numbered; but he was just not good on a game of "hide-and-seek."

This frame-up involved the whole human race. The Scripture, both Old and New Testament, has any number of frame-ups. And they are associated with a killing. Blood! Blood! It seems that God is always wanting someone else's blood.

THE FRAME-UP OF THE CRUCIFIXION

This is the greatest frame-up of them all; both Jesus Christ and Judas Iscariot. It is to be remembered that it was the scheme, according to tradition, that Jesus was to give his life for the remission of sin, and that he should be betrayed and delivered into the hands of sinful men and be crucified. But what is hard to understand is why Judas should be censured for the part he played in the scheme. We must now remember when Jesus was arrested that one of them with him attempted to defend him and struck a servant of the high priest with his sword and Jesus said to him, "How then shall the Scripture be fulfilled, that thus it must be." [42] Was it not equally true in the case with Judas? He was chosen for the purpose and Jesus had identified him at the Last Supper; he [Judas] had no choice in the

---

[41] This is from Andrew Lang's poem, "To Omar Khayyam." See John Pollen, translator, *Omar Khayyam* (London: East and West, Ltd., 1915), vi.

[42] Matthew 26: 51-54.

matter. Let us suppose that he should have backed out and refused to play his part, what then? As Jesus asked the defender, how could the scripture have been fulfilled as written?

Jesus did attempt to back out and prayed three times to avoid the crucifixion, "O my father, if it be possible, let this cup pass from me; nevertheless, not as I will but as thou will."[43]

RELIGION A MYTH

In all of my investigation, going back over ten thousand years, I have not found a religion that its claims in the main are possible, to say nothing of true or reasonable. This assertion applies to the present as well as the past. I do not wish to appear unreasonable! That is what I am striving to get away from, "the unreasonable, the impossible!!" Pick your religion and take three cardinal points to test and they will not bear the light of fair and honest investigation.

Let us begin at home. Take the Biblical account of creation, that the world was made in six days, and other accounts fixes the age at about 6,400 years, while all scientists say it is over 100,000,000 million years old.

Next we will consider the creation of man and woman. First we have a man without either father or mother, then we have a woman without a mother, next we have a man without a father. Will Biology or Anthropology or any laws of Nature support these claims? If it [the Biblical story of creation] is true, why is it not taught in our universities?

Now we will consider the story of the Deluge, supposed to be 2347 B.C. and said to have destroyed all mankind except six persons. Physics teaches us that all the moisture that was ever upon the earth is still here. We know there is not enough to have inundated the earth.

---

[43] Matthew 26:39.

Science will not support the story. I cannot think that any well-informed person believes it.

CREATION: Cause and Effect

Let us now consider the creation of the Earth and Mankind, its purpose and failures.

In debating this subject, let's be fair and apply the same reason to it that we would to any other subject of importance.

Shall we assume a divine creator that could do all things and do them well, at least to his own liking? If so, from what followed, it would seem such an assumption is far from right. The man that he made in his own likeness disobeyed the first command; he ate the forbidden fruit and thus became wise. Would he [God] be pleased to look down on a world of morons? However, he pronounced a curse upon man and his posterity. I can defend Adam in this transgressing by saying, "I had rather labor and be wise than to be an idle fool."[44] Adam did keep one command however, "Go forth, multiply, and replenish the earth."[45]

According to the report, the world moved along for some two thousand years and man continued more rebellious and sinful, until God became much grieved and repented that he had made man.

"If the Potter's hand should slip and the pot should drop?
Which is to blame, the potter or the pot?"[46]

---

[44] I have not been able to find this quote attributed to anyone else. Perhaps it is original with Arthur.

[45] There is no verse in the *Bible* written exactly the way Arthur quoted it, nor was the command directed at Adam, but it is very close to three verses in Genesis, two of which are directed at Noah. One reads: "And God blessed Noah and his sons, and said unto them, Be fruitful, and multiply, and replenish the earth." See Genesis 9:1 and 9:7. A similar quote is directed at the creatures of the earth, not human beings. See Genesis 1:22.

[46] I have been unable to find the source of this quote.

Did this all-wise creator not know what he was about as to the results? That he was contriving to bring grief to himself and damn a world for all time, which he subsequently would destroy by reason of its failure? That he in a second tryout would sacrifice his own son and again fail? I said "again fail." It is hard for me to believe that as to dissension, strife, disorder, and bloodshed, the world was not in a worse condition prior to the days of the flood than it is today. I think the reader will admit the same.

Why doesn't God stop this war [WWII]? As he stopped the sun in days past that the battle might continue?

I am wondering now what reaction this article will have on the reader if he or she is orthodox.

No, we have no account of him [God] acting as a mediator, but he has always been strong for agitation. "Have no mercy, spare none, not ever the sucklings at the breast." Read it yourself! The book is at your hand.

IS PRAYER ANSWERED?

If prayer was answered[47] as we have believed and has been promised in the Scriptures, there would be no reason why we could not put every hospital in the land out of commission in a single day. "Ask and ye shall receive."[48] Whatever may occur subsequent to the petition, the request has nothing whatever to do with it. Why do we believe upon one failure after another? It is Fear! Superstition. The same thing that makes the Negro halt his steps when a black cat crosses his path; fear chills his

---

[47] Arthur's definition of "answered" implies "answered in the affirmative."

[48] Again, although the *Bible* does not say this exactly the way Arthur quotes it, he is very close. Matthew 7:7-8 reads (a little repetitiously): "Ask, and it shall be given you; seek, and ye shall find; knock, and it shall be opened unto you. For everyone that asketh receiveth; and he that seeketh findeth; and to him that knocketh it shall be opened."

blood and freezes him on the spot.[49] If it was possible to kill that nerve of fear, the source of superstition, your faith in prayer would wilt like a flower cut at the stem. I told you at the outset in explaining primitive man, that religion was born of Fear and is at the root of Superstition. Not knowing there is nothing to fear, we strive to escape the wrath of something mightier than ourselves. I could "hang my harp on the willows and weep."[50] Poor man in his imaginative mind has built himself a tyrant God and a burning Hell to torture himself through this passport of life.

Having here laid a foundation indirectly, we will next take up the subject of prayer primarily.

For the first concrete example of the test of prayer, let us take the prayer of the Son to the Father on the Mount of Olives just before the Crucifixion. See Matthew, chapter 26, verse 39. "O my Father, if it be possible, let this cup pass from me; nevertheless, not as I will, but as thou will." From what subsequently happened, would you say his prayer was answered? Some want to say "yes" and lean on the addendum, "Thy will be done and not mine." I say no. If the last words were the request, he might as well have not gone up there. However, let's make a comparison. We will suppose that a man applies at a bank for the loan of money and he approaches the cashier with "I am in need of a thousand dollars, will you lend it but use your own judgment." And he leaves with empty hands

---

[49] For his time and place (racially-segregated Texas in the mid-1940s), I think Arthur was probably much more open-minded about race relations than most people. Therefore, I honestly don't think he realized, when he wrote this sentence, that it could be construed as a racist comment or at the very least, stereotyping. There were almost certainly a lot of white people who also held to this superstition, as well as many African-Americans who did not.

[50] Again, Arthur is using a quote that I cannot find exactly the way he writes it. This may be an allusion to a popular song, "I'll Hang My Heart on a Willow Tree," or it could be a reference to a Biblical verse, "We hanged our harps upon the willows." See Psalm 137:2.

and empty pockets. Would you say his request had been complied with? Then the president of the bank asks the cashier what the man wanted. "He made a request for a thousand dollars." Then the president inquires, "Did you comply with his request." The cashier answers, "No."

Listen, for I am speaking in a whisper. If Jesus went off to be alone, who knows what he said?

Now on this important subject we will take a long flight through space and time, back to our country, America, in 1944.

Have we the same God as in the past, and are his promises still valid?

We will take for our check one of the most important events of recent times. Prior to the D-Day invasion of Europe by our sea, land, and air forces [on June 6, 1944], the papers had been giving warning as to what to expect and President Roosevelt announced that at warning by sirens, all citizens were requested to engage in prayer for the success and safety of the soldiers with such gigantic tasks at hand. But what happened was the convoys sailed across the English Channel to the shores of France in the face of one of the worst storms of the season. Ernie Pyle (reporter) said the next day the beach and bay were strewn with wreckage and dead men, and the casualties from the storm far exceeded those from the enemy's guns.[51]

I am assuming that many people prayed, the clergy especially, and doubtless Roosevelt himself, and knowing man as I do, I would say that most of those soldiers died with a prayer on their lips. Would you say that the prayers were answered? In addition to this, weather conditions have been against the Allies almost every day since.

---

[51] I've looked for Pyle's column, where he is supposed to have written that the dead from the storm exceeded deaths from enemy guns, but haven't found it. It may be that Arthur obtained that statistic from a different report. He is right however; stormy weather certainly did create many problems during the invasion.

Now I presume my reader will point to the gains that have been made and the victories that have been gained. But I assure you it has been the belch of the cannon and the sacrifice of sweat and blood that gained the day. Let the soldiers drop their guns and engage in prayer and see what happens. Hitler would want no better opportunity.

Now I will take another step forward into my own abode and inject myself into the discussion and subject myself as evidence of my sincerity. I am now domiciled in a convalescent home, in a large apartment on the corner that we refer to as "the big house." There are sixteen old women patients, who I dare say all believe and all pray. Next door, a one-story cottage houses five men, including myself.[52] They too believe and pray, except one.[53] We read the papers and discuss topics of the day, the war, politics, and sometimes even merge into religion. A few evenings past, we all sat on the porch talking as usual. From previous conversations I had already been spotted as a heretic, and one who is a paralytic on one side, in the midst of the subject said to me, "Don't you believe in prayer?" I frankly admitted that I did not. He replied, "I think anyone that doesn't believe is in a bad fix." I responded by saying that it appeared to me that some that *do* believe in prayer are also in a bad fix. Then I said, "Listen and be reasonable for one time in your life. Do you remember the passage of Scripture that says 'if you have as much faith as that of a mustard seed, ye can move mountains?' Now your affliction is your mountain, let's see you move it. The first thing that you did was to utter a prayer and you prayed since. Am I right?" He refused to answer. Then I said, "I am going to make you all an offer that will settle the question in your minds for all times and

---

[52] As pointed out in a footnote in the Introduction, Arthur was probably residing in East Dallas, at the Garret Park Convalescent Home, 1413 N. Garrett Avenue, when he wrote this essay.
[53] Obviously, Arthur is referring to himself.

I furthermore submit myself as a test. I will take the place of the guinea pig. I have one eye with perfect vision; the other is entirely gone with cataract. Now you all tonight engage in prayer that the sight of my good eye be removed, that I wake in the morning totally blind." "Oh no," they exclaimed, "We wouldn't want to do that." "Don't fear," I said, "I will not be in the least danger. But if you have any scruples, just swop eyes and pray that my blind eye be restored to sight and see what happens. Don't you think that God would back you up in a test of his own word? 'Oh ye of little faith.' If you cannot move the mountain, there is one of two things self-evident. Either you have not faith of a 'mustard seed' or the claim is not true. Take your choice." (They all got mad and that broke up the party.)

PRAYER
Pray to the Tradition God

It has always been hard for me to accept the common viewpoint that man had to assume a humiliated trend of mind on his knees to ask a favor of the Divine Creator, and for things he should justly have by his own effort. "Lord, give us this day our daily bread." It seems that man must be under a spell of inferior complex before he is in condition of position to approach the Lord. And too, he must acquire a dialect different from that used in everyday life, such as "Thou knowest" and the like. Then we belittle ourselves: "We are no more than worms of the dust." Then we praise him: "Thou are the Kingdom, the Power, and the Glory." These of course are quoted but we engage in many others of our own composition just as ludicrous.

I have just read a story of the King of Siam, and how he compelled subjects to crawl to his feet on their hands and knees. Of course kneeling is not quite so much but it goes far in that direction. I cannot imagine any high-grade character of intelligence, either man or God who would require any such humiliation, just to please the vanity of one in power. Would you require such a thing of a servant or your child? If the God be superior to us, He should prove it in his dealing with us.

THE PRIESTHOOD, PAST AND PRESENT

This subject is so ancient, so vast and so varied, that one hardly knows where to begin or how to deal with it. If you tell the truth, you are sure to get into trouble, for the truth is sometimes a painful thing. But Huxley once said, "I would rather have a painful fact than a pleasant fallacy."[54]

I have used the word Priesthood trying to find a title that would embody the functioning of all ecclesiastical orders regardless of denominations. Perhaps Priestcraft would have been more appropriate, for most assuredly churches of all kinds are institutions and are set up and are operating on business principles providing a livelihood for men and women, amassing property that provides incomes to further its purposes, which is not fair to the state.[55]

The official functioning of these different organizations are too varied and numerous here to go into detail but they all have two things in common, "a means for a lucrative living and the reverence of his fellow man."[56]

The organization and operation of the different churches are very much like that of an army or state. They each have their commanders-in-chief, secretaries of different departments, generals, captains, and so on down the line, even to the WACS.[57]

---

[54] See previous footnote about this quote.
[55] I am not sure what Arthur means here unless he is referring to the fact that church property is generally not taxed.
[56] This quote appears to be from a book or an article of some kind but I have not been able to locate it.
[57] Women's Army Corps.

THE ORGANIZATION
The Catholic Church is the best organized of them all in the western world and has the best discipline.

THE PRELATES
The Pope, cardinals, bishops, priests, sisters, nuns, etc.

THE PROTESTANTS
Bishops, ministers, elders, preachers, deacons, etc.

JEWS
Rabbis.

MOHAMMEDANS
Caliph.

In a comparison of these ecclesiastical orders with that of an army, you can pick out a representative for almost every office of the army. Example: The Pope or bishop serves as commander-in-chief, the cardinals as Secretary of War, the priests as generals in the field, captains, and etc., while the Sisters of Charity would take the place of nurses, very appropriately. The priest would also fill the place of a surgeon or chaplain, and sometimes do. The Member takes the place of the Taxpayer for he never knows what goes with his money.

"Hope springs eternal in the human breast
Man never is, but always is to be blest."[58]

I have not picked the Catholic Church for any particular reason; the same will apply to the Protestant as well.

---

[58] This quote is from the English poet Alexander Pope.

THE METHODS OF PROCEDURE

In addition to what has been said I wish to call attention to the methods of that practiced by the churches and by the war ministers. To do this properly, I will have to take a step backward into the shadows of the Dark Ages. I have mentioned those years of shame time and time again. I wish I could inspire a few readers to investigate them—hideous nights of human misery; find the causes and place the blame, and call upon religion to take the rap.

In the first century A.D., Ptolemy at Alexandria had told the public what they wanted to believe, that the world was the center of the universe, and the sun and stars were speeding around it. Their minds were already pregnant with superstition and susceptible to anything but the truth. Christianity swept in. This fitted their teaching; hadn't Elijah commanded the sun to stand still?

The Nicene Council sat in 325 A.D. and had accepted the *Bible* as true and inspired. These were the birth pains of the Dark Ages. The twilight deepened until the fifth century and all lights went out in Europe.

We now can but wonder what the status of the western religious world would be today had the Nicene Convention turned thumbs down on the *Bible*. Who knows, I wonder."

But there was not a chance for it to miss; superstition was too deeply rooted and this old Hindu myth had been told and retold round the world too often; it is fitted into the credulous mind too well; they just couldn't pass the chance. So as it stands today, 34.2% of the civilized world accepts the verdict.[59]

Under the rule of Constantine the Christian religion blossomed and bloomed like a green bay tree. It dominated the habits and thoughts of civil life. It assessed

---

[59] This must be the percentage of Christians in the world in 1944, which today (2015) is about 33%; not much changed.

taxes for its share of your earnings. Tithing was compulsory; the church must be paid. Its arms went out like an octopus and embraced state affairs; rulers were not exempt, a request from the Church was as a command to the State. All learning was in the hands of the priests and they dealt it out sparingly. To keep their subjects submissive they must be kept in ignorance. There were some exceptions however, for some priests deviated from the rule. Copernicus was a monk but he loved science better than the church and paid for it by being ostracized. Religion has hated and feared Science in all ages, for it disproves its claims. As a result, the eclipse of the Dark Ages was on, learning was stigmatized as an insult to God. All wisdom was in the *Bible*. To attempt to cure the sick was an insult to the Deity. All Europe was a cesspool of plague and contagion; thousands died with the name of God mumbling on their lips.

THE INQUISITION

In the meantime, the Inquisition was in full power; charges of heresy were rife, for the smallest word dropped, or the act of irreverence of the Holy See, charges were filed the severest punishment inflicted, even to the burning at a stake. The Inquisition operated exactly like Hitler's Gestapo, or the Dies Committee.[60] They snooped around in crowds and listened for a word that might be dropped from a skeptic, for a word brought them by a lay member. And to be accused was equivalent to being convicted. If the offender had property, it was divided into three parts; one part went to the church and one to the state, and one part went to the head of the Inquisition. This night of darkness hovered over Europe for a period of more than three centuries and the shadows of the aftermath prevailed for another three hundred, and the effects are still visible.

---

[60] This was the popular name of the House Un-American Activities Committee when it was chaired by Congressman Martin Dies from 1938 to 1944.

They even invaded our "dear" United States, and as late as 1635 Mary Dyer and two Quakers were hanged in Boston for "heresy." Cotton Mather conducted the inquisition; Governor Endicott pronounced the sentence. Notwithstanding that the Puritans had sailed across the waters in search of religious freedom, they straightaway preferred charges against those who did not believe as they did. [61]

PROPANGANDA

The preacher in the pulpit hands you out a sermon of "Propergander." FEAR is his long suit. If he can succeed in getting you alarmed with some terrible impending danger, he's got you. When fear makes contact with superstition, it forms the sparkplug that ignites the emotions, and you are blown up. I have seen the victims fall prone; others jump up and sling their arms in frenzy and shout, "I am saved! I am saved! My sins have been forgiven!" In this state of mind he goes up and gives his hand and the preacher says a little ceremony and he is a full-fledged member of a mythical order with a life certificate for wrong doing if he prays and keeps his dues paid.

THE LEAFLETS

Leaflets of propaganda are distributed. At a corner drugstore where I get my *Reader's Digest*, a lady clerk, whom I had previously talked to, handed me a leaflet. I here quote some of its headlines:

"FOR THOSE WHO CARE"
"Would you care to know how to be saved? Would you like to be sure you are saved?"

---

[61] Arthur makes a slight mistake here. Mary Dyer first came to Massachusetts in 1635 but was not executed until 1660, although it is true that Endicott pronounced sentence. If by the "Inquisition" Arthur means the Salem Witchcraft Trials, he is right about Cotton Mather.

It follows with a string of questions and answers revolving around your accepting the story of the Crucifixion. But suppose you cannot believe that killing a Jew some two thousand years ago has any bearing on our state of being in an afterlife (if there be such). Suppose our reason will not permit our minds to accept the claim of the Jew being the "Savior" of the World, when we consider that history gives account of various others dating back over a thousand years before the advent of the Christians' claim. (I here stop to ask a question: Is personal opinion voluntary?) If the question were put to me I would say "No!" I must have evidence supporting the claim or least Science and Nature showing it possible. I mean an intelligent opinion.

SACRED BOOKS

The *Vedas*

In dealing with Hinduism we must bear in mind that Brahma is the great God; although they had thousands of gods, the "Great Brahma" was the god of all gods. As most all religions have one personality, the same applies to Brahmanism. So far as we can investigate, this wonderful religion, embracing 14.3% of the civilized world, had its concept in one Veda, at a date so remote that history does not reveal. In fact, it doubtless existed perhaps thousands of years before written history. *Veda* was in the vanguard of religious thought; it was the first to give us the concept of a human "soul." But like all religions that were to follow, its teachings were not good and uplifting. It was responsible for the caste system and created a hell to punish all who do not do thus and so. Max Muller claims the *Rig-Veda* to be the oldest religious concept in the known world.

The *Vedas* were written in four parts or books. The first *Rig-Veda* consists of one thousand and ten hymns, celebrating blessings of God. The *Sama-Veda* are hymns of lesser importance. The *Yajar-Veda* gives

28

formulary of observance for keeping sacrifices. The *Atharva-Veda* deals with blessings, charms, and maledictions, etc. This old book was first written in Sanskrit, now a dead language.

The *Pitakas* or Basket

Gautama the Buddha was born in the north of Bengal between 600 B.C. and 500 B.C. He belonged to the ruling classes of the country. He was rich and handsome and married to a beautiful wife. He was the father of one child. In spite of his high station in life and wealth, he was constantly brooding over the thoughts of old age, of sickness and death and the unknown future after death. At about thirty years of age he cut off his long locks, the sign of his high caste, and began the study of all the Brahman cults. Through his study and experiences he attained "perfect wisdom of the Buddha" and began preaching over north India. He died in 472 B.C. Buddhism has spread to many parts of the globe and its doctrine now claims 28.6% of the civilized world.

The *Pitakas* was first written in Pali, the language spoken by the common people of India, now a dead language.

H. G. Wells in *The Outline of History* said of the gospel of Buddha: "The teaching of Gautama is now being made plain to us…and it is beyond all dispute the achievement of one of the most penetrating intelligences that the world has ever known."

THE HAMMURABI CODE

Second to the *Vedas*, the Hammurabi Code is the oldest book of law in the world. It is the proclamation of the Babylonian King Hammurabi, who reigned from 2123 to 2080 B.C. We obtained the old code from a pillar originally erected in the temple at Sippara, near Baghdad, where it remained until about 1176 B.C., when the monarch Shutruk-Nakhunte overran Babylonia and removed the monument to Sussa in Persia.

NOTE: It is a question as to this old code being the oldest book of law, for the *Rig-Veda* dates back to possibly 3500 B.C. and was taught many centuries before it was written. It is here to be remembered that it was *Veda* that was responsible for Brahmanistic[62] teaching of Hinduism, and from a careful investigation you will find that every moral code or religious concept had its origin in Hinduism. The laws of Manu, about 1100 B.C., were a shoot off the old Vedic text, which also contains many of the same laws as that of Hammurabi and the Mosaic. If you will examine the Hammurabi Code you will find in it many paragraphs that are verbatim (word-for-word) as that of the Mosaic law, which comes to us some 1,670 years later, even if it was written directly after Moses' death, 1612 B.C.

But let it be remembered that the Jews did not return from their captivity in Babylonia until 836 B.C. or 1,076 years after the death of Moses. So you will observe that they *did* have contact with the Hammurabi Code. And for the sake of argument, the Code is 1,670 years older than the Pentateuch. But the evidences are that Moses got it from the same sources Hammurabi did—the Hindus. It all came out of Brahmanism through the *Veda's Rig-Veda*, and the Laws of Manu, which is a shoot off the Vedic text.

THE LAWS OF MANU

We will now discuss the Laws of Manu, which is a branch of the old Vedic tree of Brahmanism. Brahma is the same to the Hindus as Jehovah is to the Jews. As before mentioned, very likely every religion in the civilized world can be traced back to Hindu mythology in the Valley of the Ganges.

---

[62] This is apparently Arthur's own word, which I cannot find in the dictionary.

The Manu Law begins with the story of Creation, which does not differ much from the fables told in other mythologies, including Genesis. It seems that all of these old myths had their origin with the Hindus and were passed around from one country to another on down the line and accepted without question, even until this day.

The Laws of Manu were written in Sanskrit, as most of the sacred books were, and consist of twelve parts or books, too long to deal with here in detail.

The second book is the law pertaining to the Priesthood, showing their duty, training and their function, etc.

The third book is less important; it deals principally with the customs and rituals.

The fourth book refers to morals and moral laws. "Let him say what is true, but let him say what is pleasant."[63] "Let him say 'well and good' or let him say well only."

The fifth book relates largely to what shall be eaten, when, where, and how. "Not a mortal exists more sinful than he who without oblation to the manes (or the gods) desiring to enlarge his own flesh with the flesh of another creature."

The sixth book of laws sets forth the duties of worship, the modes, etc.

The seventh book pertains to the duties of rulers, kings, or priests and teachers in general.

The eighth book of law is a code for the preservation of rights of differences.

---

[63] This entire quote is: "Let him say what is true, let him say what is pleasing, let him utter no disagreeable truth, and let him utter no agreeable falsehood; that is the eternal law." I imagine that Arthur would not agree with the first three-fourths of this law, which contradicts the sentiments of Thomas H. Huxley, previously quoted herein. One wonders, however, if you are not supposed to "utter" a "disagreeable truth" or an "agreeable falsehood," then what *can* you say?

The tenth book deals with tribal rights, castes, etc.

The eleventh relates to rights of penances and a whole host of things in general.

The twelfth book (and last) deals exclusively with the doctrines of transmigration and future rewards, punishments, etc.[64]

The Laws of Manu were written perhaps about 1100 B.C. However, this old book of law must have been in use long before the above date from the fact that Krishna, who said to written his laws about 1200 B.C., quotes the Manu Laws. But as Max Muller has well said:

"Dates in India prior to established dates that have a variance of a century or two are not to be despised."[65]

THE LAWS OF KRISHNA

In the laws of Krishna, there is to be found the lethal interpretation of Hindu mythology as contained in the Vedic text. Krishna was one of the many saviors to visit the earth and the most striking story parallel with that of Jesus Christ to be imagined. Still, he dates back to 1200 B.C. His birth had been prophesied, one to be born of Brahma who would break the fetters of India. King Cansa issued an edict and destroyed all male children in an effort to destroy Krishna. He had a forerunner named Bali Rama; his mother was a Holy Virgin, her name Maia; his earthly father was a worker in wood, his heavenly father was represented as a spirit (Holy Ghost). The father of Krishna was warned that the life of the child was sought by the king and he [the earthly father] with the mother fled to Mathura, where Krishna was born on the 25th day of December. He was attended by the shepherds and wise

---

[64] The reader may have noticed by now that Arthur skipped the first and ninth books. I conjecture that this was just an oversight and not deliberate.

[65] I have been unable to ascertain which one of Muller's many works contains this quote.

men came bringing spices, gold, and myrrh to his cradle, to worship him. They were from the East, a star led the way. Krishna retired to the wilderness for meditation and prayer at twenty years of age, emerging at twenty-two. He was called "The Savior of the World," "The Son of God." He was claimed to have been from the beginning and was sent from a heavenly father to rid the world of demons and sin, and to convert it to righteousness.

Krishna abolished the caste system and washed his disciples' feet. He warned his disciples of his death and had a last supper with his twelve disciples. He was accused and tried for teaching false creeds and was crucified between two thieves.

Krishna broke with the old Brahman and Manu laws much the same as Jesus did with the old Mosaic law, and the teachings of his new code was very much in line with the New Testament.

When we compare the above with the reading of the *New Testament*, a space between of 1,200 years, it brings us up with a shock. How did it happen? And we begin to check. We remember that the Jews, during their sojourn in Egypt, were exposed to this old Vedic and Hindu mythology, as both the Hammurabi Code and Mosaic Law bear evidence. The story must have appealed to a great many. The story of Zoroaster on the island of Crete was copied from that of Krishna. Kersey Graves, in his remarkable book, gives account of sixteen saviors of the world born on the 25th of December, of a virgin mother, and crucified. It looks suspicious to say the least.

A painting showing the crucifixion of Krishna is to be found in the British Museum.[66]

---

[66] If this is true, it is not displayed on the British Museum website, but it should be noted that the museum contains literally thousands of rare artifacts from ancient times that are also not included there.

THE ZEND-AVESTA

One point of great interest about this book is that no other document in existence is written in the same language, the "Zend," now a dead language.

The *Zend-Avesta* is a canon consisting of five books ascribed to Zoroaster, said to have been written on 12,000 cowhides. His creed patterned the Brahmanic theology. The fable ran as follows: At the beginning, there existed two spirits, Ormud (God), who created all things good, and Ahrimana (Devil), who created all things evil. Ormud is light, life, law, order, and truth. Ahrimana is darkness, falsehood, and evil. It was dual system in perpetual conflict, much the same as represented in Christian mythology, and apparently had its origin at the same fountain source, Brahmanism as taught by Veda, Manu, and Krishna.

The *Zend-Avesta* is the Persians'. Avesta means text. Zend means commentary.

You will perceive that Zoroaster represents an off-shoot from the Vedic teaching of ancient India, or the Hindu religion.

CONFUCIUS

Confucius, the Chinese sage, was born at Lu in 551 B.C. Some think he lived at a much earlier date, but we cannot say.

The *Prophecies of Confucius* was not regarded by the Chinese as being an inspired book but rather a book of law or moral behavior between men, much as the *Bible* was prior to the Nicene Council. But in the event of time, it was accepted more seriously and gradually became the basis for a religion. It [the *Prophecies of Confucius*] contains nine of the Mosaic Ten Commandments and the golden rule, "Whatsoever you would that men should do unto you, do you likewise to them,"[67] and many other

---

[67] See the New Testament of the *Bible*, Matthew 7:12 and Luke 7:31.

moral precepts found in the laws of Manu and Krishna. Again we fancy we see the reflection of Hinduism.

When Confucius was three years old, his father died, leaving him and his mother very poor. When old enough, he had charge of the public store for a while, and then he had charge of public herds. At twenty-two years of age he began teaching. In 501 B.C. a new ruler made him governor of Lu, his old home town. He made many reforms but in the event of years found himself in disfavor with the ruler, after which he traveled for twelve years with his disciples, teaching as he went, but later a new ruler recalled him to Lu, where he [Confucius] died in 479 B.C., thus ending a busy and turbulent life.

THE ILIAD AND THE ODYSSEY

Greece has no sacred book. The *Iliad* and the *Odyssey* by the blind bard, Homer, is the nearest to that epoch.

The Greeks bring to us as a cornerstone of their literature and their belief, the typical epics, the Iliad and the Odyssey; poems of action and prowess; the great deeds of their ancestors and heroes were worthy antagonists for the gods themselves.

The imagination of East India has evolved a great change and the greatest dreams of the Gods of *Veda* and Manu have long since taken possession of their superstitious minds and have produced many gods. Egypt had over three thousand gods and Herodotus said he could trace every Grecian god to that of Egypt. So again we see the footprints of the Hindu; and if you keep track, you will see its foot on the doorstep of the western home.

The Iliad and the Odyssey were written about 850 B.C.

THE ORIGIN OF *THE BIBLE*

The *Bible* as we know it is not as old as many people think (that is, the compiling of it) but we have no record of the date of the manuscripts from which it was compiled. The first books, attributed to Moses and sometimes referred to as the Pentateuch, must have been written many years after Moses' death. Authorities differ, however, as to the possible date. Some say 900 years while others claim that they were written as late as 1,210 years after the death of Moses.

COMPILING *THE BIBLE*

When Cyrus, King of Persia, captured Babylonia in the year 538 B.C., he did it by bribing the Jewish gatekeepers with the promise of their freedom for letting him through the gates. They did so and he made good his promise. (It is to be remembered that the Jews were captives in Babylonia at this time.) When King Cyrus liberated the Jews he told them to go back to their country and collect all their old manuscripts, songs, and folklore, and make themselves a book of their own. They collected 366 rolls of parchment; they were called "vollos" (by the way, that is where we get the word "volume."[68])

These Jews in Babylonia were living under the Hammurabi law, likely a copy of the old Manu Law brought over from Egypt by the Children of Israel. This will account for the similarity of the Mosaic Law and the Hammurabi Code. It was quite natural, when they made themselves a book, that they would inject a code of laws common to that under which they had been accustomed.

After collecting the 366 rolls of manuscripts, they appointed seventy-two scholars (they called them scribes). They were not supposed to be inspired but to select from this collection the books best suited for their new book. The called it "The Book of Law." This was sometime after 538 B.C. When a roll came under discussion, they voted on the merits of it; some books got in by only one vote.

---

[68] I have been unable to verify this claim but it sounds plausible.

They finally decided on sixty-two books that now comprise our old *Bible*, or the Jewish Book of Law. The other 304 books were discarded and referred to as the Apocrypha.

Things drifted along for more than eight hundred years, and in the interim, the *New Testament* had been added, and some of the Jewish people had begun to regard the book more seriously, claiming it was of inspired origin. The Jewish nation was torn with dissension, so Constantine called an assembly to fix an agreement on certain doctrinal points and books that the Jewish Church refused to accept as canonical or true. While it was possible for all to take action in the council, the main body of the Jewish Church refused to take action with them, resulting in having the New Testament attributed to Jesus the Christ, and he was raised to the attitude of a Messiah or a God.

This council, called in 325 A.D., at Nicaea, accepted these books as true and inspired.

This council, it is to be understood, dealt with the books of the New Testament only. The old book of law had been considered as a revelation from God for about 400 years.

THE NEW TESTAMENT

It has been said that we would not have known Socrates except through Plato, and it is perhaps equally true that we would not have known Jesus except for St. Paul. I have sometimes debated with myself if we have not a more Paul-like religion than a Christian religion in view of the fact that Paul never met Jesus. Paul was born about the same date as Jesus, 3 B.C., some say 6 B.C. In the year 1 A.D. Jesus was between three and four years old.

The Epistle of St. Paul, written between 50 and 60 A.D. is probably genuine, but the other books seem to be more or less in doubt, being identified as E. J. Q., etc. I will not take them up in detail, assuming that the reader is posted along these lines if he or she be a Christian. Everyone should know the background of their religion.[69]

The latest of these books were written about 70 A.D. and the Nicene Council that passed upon them as inspired books was held in 325 A.D., or not until 255 years later. And the Old Jewish Book of Law went some 400 years with no one suspecting of it having divine origin.

WHY JESUS BROKE WITH THE OLD LAW

When Moses led the Israelites out of Egypt, he either did not take them all or some of them found their way back, for when Alexander the Great overran Egypt about 350 B.C. there was quite a host of them still there. He took a large number of them and settled them at Alexandria. They became students and disciples of Essenian teachers, who were leaders of a sect known as Essenians, the leading power in Alexandria, and the Jews readily became converts. Jesus, of course, was not one of this clan but his ancestors were. These Essenians were a protestant shoot off the old Manu Law, the same as Luther and Knox were off the Catholic Church. When they came back to Palestine to meet their brethren from Babylonia, they found themselves divided into two different cults. It was but natural that Jesus should take to the parent cult, and he began to teach and to preach. His doctrine was quite a departure from that of the old Jewish Book of Law, "The Bible." So we see the Jew bringing Paul before the Judge Gallio, saying, "This man persuadeth me to worship God contrary to the law" (an infidel).[70]

---

[69] I think Arthur was taking a huge "leap of faith" here. It appears to me that except for a relative few, Christians are woefully ignorant of the background of their religion, too lazy to look into it and just accepting whatever their preacher or Sunday School teacher tells them they ought to do or to believe.

[70] Acts 18:18-23.

A good man he [Paul] was. As one man has said, "He was branded as a heretic, crucified as an infidel. If I had lived in those days, I would have been his friend."[71]

Christianity embraces most of the western world. About 550,000,000 people, or 34.2 percent of civilization, broke up into many creeds, over 400 Protestants alone, to say nothing of other malgations.[72]

THE *KORAN*

Mohammed, the founder of Islam, was a most remarkable man. He was born at Mecca, Arabia in the year 570 A.D. His early life was spent in poverty, partly as a shepherd, sometimes as a camel driver in the caravan of a rich widow fifteen years his senior. A while after his marriage, he spent his time as a merchant, but largely in lonely meditation. Christianity and Judaism both prevailed in Arabia at the time. His first religious revelation was received from Gabriel when he [Mohammed] was forty years old. These revelations continued at intervals and were collected and written down after his death, forming the *Koran*.

At first, Mohammed was regarded as a harmless maniac, but as his followers increased and his attacks on the old religions became more severe, the people rose against him and his whole clan was outlawed. He decided to flee to the City of Medina, where he died in 622 A.D.

The *Koran* is founded on the *Bible* and the Mosaic Law revised. He acknowledged Moses and the prophets but claims that Mohammed is the latest and greatest prophet of them all.

This book, like all other religions, has strongly the earmarks of Hinduism.

---

[71] I have unfortunately been unable to find the source of this quote.
[72] Arthur seems to have just made up this word but I think his meaning is clear.

THE BOOK OF MORMON or LATTER DAY SAINTS

As all sacred books have their sponsor, the *Book of Mormon* has it in one Joseph Smith, born in Vermont in 1805. He was fifteen years old when he had his first vision. I cannot do better than to quote his own story of his experience, taken from the book itself, which is as follows in part:

"While I was thus in the act of calling upon God, I discovered a light appearing in my room, which continued to increase until the room was lighter than at noonday, when immediately a personage appeared at my bedside, standing in the air, for his feet did not touch the floor."[73]

He continues with the description of the personage, too lengthy to follow.

In this vision he received his call to the work of a prophet. This was followed by a revelation of a place where he would find a metallic plate on which was engraved the history and religions of the ancient inhabitants of America.[74] In 1827 this record was put into his hands together with two transparent stones fastened to the rim of a bow, somewhat like a pair of spectacles, but larger. This peculiar instrument was called the "Urim and Thummim of Interpreter" by the means of which he translated the unknown language of the records. Three persons were permitted to see the originals and in a miraculous manner; while eight testified that Smith showed them the book or plates.

Of course we hardly expect those of Christian faith to admit any sacredness to these reported visions. But in all fairness to the subject, are they less reasonable than the Mosaic story of his command at the burning bush? Or

---

[73] This is from the *History of Joseph Smith, History of the [Mormon] Church*, vol. 1, chapters 1-5, verse 30.
[74] Arthur's account is not entirely accurate. Smith allegedly found several golden plates, not just one.

of his receiving the Ten Commandments on the tablets of stone? ("Oh consistency thou art a jewel."[75])

The Mormons constantly ran afoul of law and public indignation on account of their heresy, much the same as Jesus did. Finally, Joseph Smith and his brother Hyrum were thrown in jail June 27, 1844. Both he and his brother were shot to death through the windows of the jail by a howling crowd from the outside. ("Woe be unto the non-conformer."[76])

Now this path begins to dwindle to a pig trail. Still we have Mrs. Baker-Eddy with her "Christian Science," and Amie McPherson, Alexander Dowie, Father Divine, and scores of others yet to come.[77]

"Who knows, I wonder?"

---

[75] This quote is usually attributed to William Shakespeare.
[76] Here's another quote for which I cannot find the source.
[77] Amie Semple McPherson was a popular American evangelist and faith healer whose heyday was the 1920s, Dowie was a nineteenth century Scottish evangelist and faith healer from Australia, and Father Divine was an African-American spiritual leader who actually claimed to be God.

DEATHS OF THE APOSTLES

<u>3 Crucified</u>
    1   Andrew was crucified in Arabia
    2   Simon was crucified in Persia
    3   Peter was crucified at Rome
<u>1 Beheaded</u>
    4   James (son of Zebedee) was beheaded at Jerusalem
<u>2 Hanged</u>
    5   Philip was hanged at Phrygia
    6   Judas Iscariot hung himself
<u>2 Killed With Lances</u>
    7   Matthew was slain with a sword in Ethiopia
    8   Thomas was slain with a lance in the East Indies
<u>4 Miscellaneous</u>
    9   James (brother of Jesus) was thrown from the pinnacle of the Temple and beaten to death with a fuller's club
    10 Bartholomew was flayed alive in Arabia
    11 Thaddeus was shot to death with arrows
    12 John died of natural causes

Paul, often an Apostle, never saw Jesus and was not present at the last supper.

Paul was beheaded at Rome.

(16) SAVIORS OF THE WORLD

BORN OF VIRGINS AND CRUCIFIED

1	KRISHNA of India
	Crucified				1200 B.C.
See Kersey Graves, p. 98
2	SAKI MUNI of the Hindus
	Crucified				600 B.C.
See Graves, p. 201
3	TRAMMUZ of Syria
	Crucified				1160 B.C.
See Graves, p. 107
4	WITOBA of the TELINGONESES
	Crucified				552 B.C.
See Graves, p. 108
5	IAC of Nepal
	Crucified				622 B.C.
See Graves, p. 108
6	HESUS of the Celtic Druids
	Crucified				843 B.C.
See Graves, p. 109
7	QUEXALCOTE of MEXICO
	Crucified				587 B.C.
See Graves, p. 109
8	QUIRINUS of Rome
	Crucified				506 B.C.
See Graves p. 110
9	AESHYLUS (PROMETHEUS)
	Crucified				547 B.C.
See Graves, p. 110
10	THULIS of Egypt
	Crucified				1700 B.C.
See Graves, p. 112
11	INDRA of Tibet
	Crucified				725 B.C.
See Graves, p. 112

| 12 | ALCESTOS of Euripides | |
| | Crucified | 600 B.C. |
See Graves, p. 113

| 13 | ATYS of Phrygia | |
| | Crucified | 1170 B.C. |
See Graves, p. 113

| 14 | CRITE of Chaldea | |
| | Crucified | 1200 B.C. |
See Graves, p. 113

| 15 | BALI of ORISSA | |
| | Crucified | 725 B.C. |
See Graves, p. 114

| 16 | METHRA of Persia | |
| | Crucified | 600 B.C. |
See Graves, p. 114

NOTE: The sixteen Saviors of the World do not include Jesus of Nazareth, crucified 33 A.D.

Kersey Graves, in this interesting collection, [78] has given biographic descriptions of each character, quoting other authors, acquainting us with those men who gave their all the same as Jesus, hoping to save the world from sin! But did they? What is your verdict?

"Who knows, I wonder?"

---

[78] Kersey Graves' book, *The World's Sixteen Crucified Saviors,* has been republished numerous times. I have unfortunately been unable to locate an edition with the same page numbers that Arthur cites here.

RELIGIONS OF THE WORLD[79]

CHRISTIANS		
CATHOLICS............	270,000,000	16.7%
PROTESTANTS.........	170,000,000	10.5%
GREEKS.................	110,000,000	7.0%
Total ..	550,000,000	34.2%

PAGANS		
MOHAMMEDANS .	220,000,000	13.6%
BRAHMANS..........	230,000,000	14.3%
BUDDHISTS..........	460,000,000	28.6%
HEATHENS............	140,000,000	8.7%
Total	1,080,000,000	65.8%

WORLD POPULATION

        1,610,000,000   As of 1926

---

[79] Arthur's failure to include the Jews was almost certainly just an oversight. Reading his work has led me to conclude that either he just couldn't type fast enough to keep up with his thoughts or he simply became fatigued, which seems more likely given his advanced age (79), when writing this essay.

BIBLICAL CHRONOLOGY

Creation according to the *Bible*	4004 B.C.
The Deluge	2348 B.C.
Abraham in Canaan	2084 B.C.
Israelites Led out of Egypt	1652 B.C.
Moses Died	1612 B.C.
Jacob and Family in Egypt	1867 B.C.
Babylon Independence	747 B.C.
Cyrus Conquers Babylon	538 B.C.
Jews Begin to Rebuild Temple	536 B.C.
Jesus the Christ Born	3 B.C.
Jesus Crucified	33 A.D.

PART TWO

"Science is my Bible. Nature is my God. To do good is my Religion. Oblivion is my Heaven."

—Arthur Babb

William Hogarth, "Credulity, Superstition and Fanaticism: A Medley" (1762).

A BIBLICAL MERRY-GO-ROUND

A PREFACE

If we must assume a Deity separate and outside the forces of nature as author of same, with unlimited power to create all things as he would have them be; we must also assume that he has the power to guide and direct the behavior of his own creation and is therefore responsible for the results. Let us suppose that Henry Ford should design and turn out a car with a defective steering gear that would riot and destroy itself, its occupants, and pedestrians on the street; where would you place the blame? Perhaps, you might say, the driver! The hand of nature is at the steering wheel and the foot of predestination is on the gas throttle. You can't deny the facts if you accept the God as revealed in the Scripture. Some might try to find a way out by placing blame of all discord on man, saying he was made perfect and given free will to choose between right and wrong, which is far from facts if the Scripture be true or reason has any value. In the Scripture we read, "There is none perfect, no not one."[80] And reason shows we succumb to the greatest attraction and call it chaos.

We can if we will, but can we will?

Why does mankind proclaim God "merciful?" Worship is inspired by fear! You may take both sacred and profane history, "if you will admit facts" and it will lead you to one conclusion.

We must consider God to be all-powerful, having the ability to do all things as he would have them be. It then follows that whatever is, or has been, is most assuredly according to his will. Ask yourself the question, "Why should he create something that he did not want? We here quote the Scripture: "All things that are were

---

[80] The actual quote, from Psalms 14:3 is "There is none that doeth good, no, not one."

made by me and without me there was not anything made that was made."[81] Therefore, he must assume the responsibility for both good and evil. There is no escape.

We must further assume that all things that are is representative of himself and what he stands for.

Now we turn to history, both sacred and profane, to see what they reveal.

Let us enter the open door and proceed down, down the ages. Following natural history and science and compare it with tradition of today.

According to Archbishop Usher's chronology, he places the date of creation at 4004 B.C. And the date of the Deluge at 2,348 B.C. Adding our calendar date to the first above, would make the world 5,949 years old.[82]

Modern science places human life on earth at not less than 2,000,000 years. How shall we account for this difference of opinion of over 1,094,000 years? These figures, however, are only quoting dates since man's appearance on earth; behind this possibly lies a night of darkness of more than 800,000,000 years.

Constantine, Emperor of Rome, called a convention at Nicaea, in the year 325 A.D. to decide the much perplexed question as to whether or not the Bible was of divine inspiration; and the Bible won out, which is not a surprise if you know your history and consider the human mind at the time and place. The "Dark Ages" was just around the corner. Christians burned each other for three hundred years, disputing over this divine book.

When conditions become normal after peace is established I wish the leading governments would get together and reconsider this matter; we should have learned something in the 1,620 years that have intervened since the Council of Nicaea met.

---

[81] Again, Arthur is close but doesn't quite get it right. The actual quote, from John 1:3 is, "All things were made by him [God]; and without him was not any thing made that was made."

[82] As of 1945; when this essay was written.

Germany laid down its arms after five years of the bloodiest contest that the world has ever known. On May 7, 1945[83] firing ceased but the wounds are left to fester. War machinery was employed more mighty than ever before, beneath the sea, on land, and in the air. The exact number of casualties will never be known, saying nothing of the suffering, woes, and heartaches yet to follow. Now we turn our face to the East and I have only to refer you to the current newspapers today, July 1945. And we strive in vain to see the ending. We read the "Peace Chart" of San Francisco, and implore God's aid, but will it come? He stopped the Sun for the battle to continue, but he has never stopped the battle. Why? The answer is, he is a war-like God, first, last, and always. We must not forget that in the beginning he created a Devil as well as man and put them in conflict, giving the Devil all the advantage, as the log-roller would say, "the long end of the stick." He seemed too enthused with human suffering that he provided a Hell in which to thrust mankind if he lost the fight; thus making his suffering perpetual in a life everlasting, that He on his throne might enjoy mankind's agony forever and ever.

BACK TO EARTH

We must not forget the Dark Ages, as one historian says, "three hundred years of shame,"[84] in which the Christian element played a major role and burned each other by the thousands. Don't ask when or where, this is addressed to those who read and have read and I am assuming that you know, possibly better than myself. Upon these assumptions we will ask ourselves, "you and I," did God foreordain this massacre? If not, why did he permit it to go on for 300 years unrestrained?

We will next step back to a period just before the birth of Jesus, until just after the Crucifixion, during the

---

[83] In the original composition Arthur wrote "April (?) 1945."
[84] I have been unable to ascertain which historian Arthur had in mind.

decline of the Roman Empire, say to 10 B.C. to 50 A.D.

Civilization was in an awful flux. Caesar had just been assassinated. The Roman Empire was divided between Marc Anthony and Octavius. Anthony held sway over Palestine and he appointed one Herod as King of Judea. Later confirmed by Octavius, it was this Herod who ordered the assassination of all the male babies of Bethlehem, hoping to get the Messiah. He [Herod] died a few years later.

Now I wish to call your attention to the atrocities of ancient Rome and see if we can place the blame. Where was God? Would he not or could he not calm the troubled waters?

We now approach the scene of the Crucifixion and a ghastly scene it is. Skipping many trials and disappointments of his life we come to a period near to the cross; Jesus had heard rumors of his accusers, his heart was rent within him. He, with a few of his disciples, came near to the Mount of Olives and withdrew himself from them, ascending the mount he fell upon his knees and prayed, saying, "O my Father, if it be possible, permit this cup to pass me. But thy will be done, not mine."[85] And we wonder why he did not want to carry out his part of the compact with the Father.

It so occurred that Jesus was brought to trial together with three others accused, two thieves and one called Barabbas, who was pardoned instead of Jesus as was intended by Pilate (this Barabbas was an uncle of St. Mark, or John Mark).

The Crucifixion was carried out according to the time and laws of the country. Jesus' mother Mary stood at the foot of the cross, trying to give comfort to her unfortunate son. He, looking down, saw her and said, "Woman, behold thy son."[86] I have always wished that he would have said "Mother" instead of "Woman," but he did

---

[85] Matthew, 26:39.
[86] John, 19:26-27.

not. Then with a loud voice he cried, "My God, my God, why hath thou forsaken me?"[87] But the only answer was the echo of his wailing cries.

How any father, to say nothing of a merciful God, could stand by without turning a hand and see a son suffer such agony, knowing that he himself was the instigator of the whole affair is beyond my sense of justice. Jesus had pled with the father to get out of the execution, but to no avail. The whole thing seems a bungle, or an unjust plot.

Let us examine the deck and see if someone has stacked the cards. It appears from all accounts that God had made such a bad job of his own handiwork, even that made after his own image, and that it behaved so much like himself, he became disgusted that he decided to do something about it. So he conceived the idea to beget a child by a Jewish girl and decreed that child should grow to manhood and be killed and it would save the world from sin. He lost the game; it didn't work. Jesus played his hand well enough but the old man didn't hold a trump and the Devil had a flush. So the game was lost and the world is still not saved from sin.

When Dr. W. Archibald Spooner of Oxford College, some hundreds of years ago, transposed a passage of Scripture, "The Lord is a loving shepherd," and made it read "The Lord is a shoving leopard,"[88] he came near to hitting the mark. This is not directed at Jesus, however, but the Scripture in general, for I feel toward the man as much as Pilate expressed himself at the trial, "I find no fault with this just man."[89] But this is not to say that I commit myself to worship.

I have always thought that God made a big mistake in not having the Devil killed instead of Jesus; it

---

[87] Matthew, 27:46.
[88] Phrases like this are called "Spoonerisms."
[89] Luke, 23:4.

would have removed much of the temptation that mankind is heir to by his influence, thus saving more souls and producing much happiness, for according to the Scripture, none is immune from his attack. We must not forget that even God was coaxed into an argument with him [the Devil], in which God killed a whole generation of people and afflicted a most innocent man, Job, to prove to the Devil he was faithful. How would you get around admitting this was not a temptation in which God succumbed to the Devil's tricks, thus punishing his most faithful servant?

If I should succumb to the lure of the Devil and kill my neighbor, I would be subject to the laws of my country, punishable by death, and according to the Scripture, my soul committed to Hell by a sin-avenging God. Honestly, have you ever denied this in your mind? I dare say you have not.

From all accounts God has always had the most uncanny way of punishing the innocent for a grudge against the offender. Take the case of old Noah, when he got drunk and stripped himself and lay down to sleep it off, his son Ham came in and seeing the amusing sight, went back and laughingly told his brothers. Shem and Japheth took garments and walked backward to cover the old man up and when he woke up with a hangover, the brothers told off on Ham. The old fellow was so mad he pronounced a curse, not on Ham as you might imagine, but on his son Canaan, saying "cursed be Canaan; a servant of servants shall he be unto his brothers."[90]

Of course we know the curse would not have been effective without supernatural aid, so as the saying goes, "we can see the snake in the woodpile."

Noah's curse was purportedly the beginning of the Negro race and slavery, and the "Jim Crow" law the aftermath.

---

[90] Genesis, 9:25.

In view of the conflict of dates and occurrence of the earth's formation, and the creation and evolution of life on it, as revealed by scientific investigation and as set forth in the Bible, it is too vast to be passed up lightly. For the aforesaid reasons, I suggest that a convention be called to reconsider the edict of the Nicene convention called by Constantine in 325 A.D., called the Council of Nicene Creed, which decreed the Bible an inspired book.

I would suggest that this new convention be composed of six university heads, six doctors, and six scientists on one side, and six heads each of three of the leading denominational churches, thirty-six men all told.

The decision of this most important convention would not be decided by vote, as you might imagine, but by a mere crucial test of facts and figures. Past history to be taken into account, the proof of the claims to be set forth, such as the age of the earth, the story of the creation, the story of the flood, etc. All evidence must be duly considered and all claims of miracles duly tested, and evidence of a soul. The effect of prayer to be tested (the above for Theology).

Doctors will be required to give lectures on the human anatomy and to explain the organs and their functions; germs and microbes causing disease, their cure and prevention; how to isolate a germ, etc.

University professors will be assigned the subject of history. They will trace the path of man from the dawn of civilization, explaining his credulities, superstitions, and worship, step by step, as they fused by contact with other tribes or nationalities, forming new cults; and to keep track of their marks up the present day.

To Science will be assigned the task to step back into a night of darkness perhaps 200,000,000 years before the dawn of written history and unfold the pages of natural history as revealed by Science, and the development of life on this planet and the evolution from the protoplasm to that of prehistoric man. Here he meets the university professor who assigns reasons for his behavior, and the doctor who explains the functioning of the structure. The circle is completed and the record is laid on the table.

I further suggest that thirty-six men of broad and liberal education be added to the assembly aforementioned. This brings the total number up to seventy-two, the same as were appointed to compile the Bible about 500 B.C., which has never been checked in the light of modern science.

The duties of the latter assigned men will be to question and cross-question the former professional bodies, each according to his profession.

Doctors will be asked to explain the function of the heart as to what it has to do with the moral concepts and behavior of the mind. They will also be asked to explain the soul, if any, as to its influence on mind and matter, and its escape form the body at death. The questioning group may deem it necessary to ask the witnesses other questions, to make sure of their knowledge of the subject that they represent.

Like questions will be asked scientists; the same to be square and on the level, not to seek to prove or disprove, but an honest search for the facts, the lack of which has separated mankind for centuries.

College professors will be asked to explain what written history reveals on subjects of importance to the various questions at hand. What it finds to support the story of creation, of the deluge of the world, the virgin birth and resurrection of a Messiah, as reported in the scriptures.

The Clergy will be next to be put on the stand, to get their version of the many questions that have been put to the physicians and scientists, and the difference in reports to be checked.

(Note: In this investigation, biblical reports are not to be taken as infallible; that is the question on trial and the purpose of the investigation.)

The questioning board would ask the Clergy when

and how we came by the book called the Bible? When was it first decreed of divine origin, and by whom? What they have to support the story of creation, the flood, and many other things that reverse all laws of nature or our present experience; to give evidence of a soul and immortality; to give a demonstration of the efficiency of prayer, something that would not occur without the petition. Example, take a man whose eyes have been removed from their socket and request that the eye be replaced with perfect vision, or a missing limb regrown with bone, flesh, and blood. Now remember these quotations, "Whatsoever ye ask of my father and believe it, it will be granted."[91] "So sayeth the Lord, 'There is nothing impossible with God.'"[92] If the request is not granted, there is just one of two conclusions, either you did not believe it, or the claim is not true; you can take your choice. We would also want the concept of Hell explained, its purposes and the author.[93]

When the conference hearing is over, all documents should be duly filed and the findings freely published, leaving it to the people as a jury and common sense as a judge. Let future generations pass the sentence. But how long, I wonder.

An Afterthought

I have just been reading in the *Reader's Digest*, "The Mystery of the Stone Towers," located in the north central part of New Mexico. Built some 700 years ago, or say about 150 years before Columbus discovered America,

---

[91] Arthur was probably thinking of John, 16:23, which actually reads: "Whatsoever ye ask in my name, that I will do."

[92] See Luke, 1:37.

[93] In this last sentence, Arthur had a blank underlined space where I have placed the word "want." I have noticed other places in the text where he sometimes seemed lost for a word and left a blank space, which he later went back and filled in using a pencil. This is the only one that was underlined, however, and the only one he did not complete.

by a colony of people that had come from somewhere to establish new homes in their quest for happiness. They built their homes in the form of forts to protect themselves against a foe. Who were these people and who were their foes? Nobody knows. Many of their bodies were found prone on the floor with the implements of death still piercing their breasts. Their prayer sticks and symbols of worship lay strewn about them. But their gods had deserted them in the hour of distress, as ever before, "My God, my God! Why hath thou forsaken me?" The thoughtful man cannot refrain from contemplating those primitive peoples' state of being in a future life if there be a soul. Can they look back upon their tower homes as the archaeologist perceives them? When Jesus was crucified some 1,245 years before, was there some provision made for those people that were destined never to hear his name? Had they a Heaven for the faithful and a Hell for the unbeliever? These questions are debatable if you believe in your own religion. I wish I had a friend, a thinker that I could talk a few subjects over with. I am now thinking of Alexander Pope:

"Awake, my St. John, leave all meaner things
To low ambitions and pride of kings:
Let us (since this life can little more supply
Than just to look about us and to die)
Expiate free o'er all this scene of man;
A mighty maze, but not without a plan;"[94]

"The man of action determines the present. But the thinker controls the future."[95]

---

[94] Arthur did not get this poem quite right in his essay. I have corrected it.

[95] This quote, the source of which Arthur failed to identify, can be found on page 43 of *Speeches by Oliver Wendell Holmes* (Boston: Little and Brown Company, 1900). Holmes actually said, "The man of action has the present, but the thinker controls the future," but Arthur's version is close enough I think.

HAS THE HUMAN BEING A SOUL?

I approach this subject in the form of a question. Regardless of how you may accept it, nevertheless it is debatable and I address myself to the reader and invite him or her to debate the question with themselves. I am also cognizant of its importance to the religious fraternity and wish to be fair to them, to myself and to the subject. I am also aware that it may cost me some friends that chance to see this perusal, but all things worthwhile are paid for with a price and I had rather give up a friend I believe to be wrong, than a principle believed to be right. I think it was Wm. H. Huxley that said, "I will not compromise with error for mental ease."[96] I can subscribe to his suggestion.

To get this subject properly in hand, I think it well to lay some ground plan as a basis to arrive at the concept of what the soul is supposed to be and its relation to the body and the spirit. This is February 24, 1945. Last Sunday a visiting minister in Dallas took for his text, "Unbelief is Cardinal Sin."[97] In discussing this subject, he separates it thus—"Three Aspects of Sin, of the Flesh, of the Soul and of the Spirit." I am not sure that this theory is representative of theologians as a whole. However, it gives us some idea and is at least a part.

Referring to the above we will consider the first suggestion, *unbelief.* The first question which arises in my

---

[96] Actually, it was Thomas H. Huxley, the English scientist and agnostic, who Arthur obviously had in mind and about whom author Elbert Hubbard wrote, saying that he [Huxley] "might never compromise with the error for the sake of mental ease, or accept a belief simply because it was pleasant; from Elbert Hubbard, *Little Journeys to the Homes of the Great*, volume 12 (New York: Wm. W. Wise & Company, 1916), 318.

[97] The minister in question was Dr. Ben H. Lacy, who gave the sermon at the First Presbyterian Church in downtown Dallas on Sunday, February 25, 1945. Arthur obviously typed the wrong date; he probably meant to write February 26. It is uncertain whether he actually heard the sermon (which seems unlikely) or if he simply read about it in the Monday, February 26 issue of the *Dallas Morning News*.

mind is what does it take to constitute a belief? Is belief voluntary? Is the intelligent mind supposed to accept a suggestion handed from another without evidence and call it belief? For my part I must say that I am incapable of doing such; if I accept a theory upon which I can base a belief, it must have supporting scientific evidence. One common mistake is made by assuming that if a man says he believes, that he is a believer. By my observation and association through a long life among many classes of men, I find they only believe a small percent of what they claim, but through fear or policy they assert, "I do believe!"

Shall we assume that the soul represents the five senses of the body as we know it in an afterlife? No one seems to have more than a vague idea. We hear mention of seeing and hearing but no mention of the other three senses. When I was a boy I tried to coax from my mother, "Mother, when do we eat?" But she did not seem to think that there was any angel food cake in Heaven. They all seem to be elusive; they hedge and beat around the bush and say it doesn't mean this or that. When you depart from the text in an attempt to interpret it, you acknowledge its fallacy. If a God was not capable of dictating his message to mankind, then we are sunk so far as the Bible is concerned. To me, it means just what it says or it doesn't mean anything.

A good deal can be assumed by listening to hymns sung in the churches. Inasmuch as they are composed by the membership, it is safe to say they represent their concept of our future condition in a life beyond the grave. Those hymns attempt to describe the pleasures that await us and the soul's reaction to them. One I remember runs as follows: "There the bright blooming flowers and their odors emitting and the leaves of the boughs in the breezes a'flitting." [98] Here we have the sense of smell mentioned, still feeling and tasting are left out; and how about sex? Now, don't get excited. It is just as much a part of the functioning of our structure and as necessary as any other organ of the body, not only for reproduction, but also for pleasure and is mentioned numerously in the Scriptures in more vulgar terms that I would like to put my mind to. I will mention at least one of the many. Turn to Numbers, chapter 31, verses 17 & 18. "Now therefore kill every male among the little ones, and kill every woman that hath known man by laying with him. But all the women children that have not known man by laying with him, keep alive for yourselves."[99] Now what kind of picture does the above suggest to your mind? Be honest, if you have read my proposal in the preceding lines that we be honest to ourselves and to the subject, and you have continued to read, then you have accepted my offer, and assuming that you will keep faith, I will ask you a question. What was the purpose of keeping all those young women? And why kill all the men? So that they would not be interfered with, of course.

In embarking with the Church we have made an investment. What does the policy propose to pay?

Another phase of this subject I would like to see

---

[98] I have been unable to find a hymn with this exact line. The closest I have been able to locate is "The Immoral Shore," sung to the tune of "The Sweet Bye and Bye," which includes this line: "And the valleys with sweet blooming flowers, send their odors afar on the breeze"; from *Hymns of the Morning* (Concord, N.H.: Charles W. Sargent, Printer, 1873), 147.

[99] It appears here that Arthur was once again quoting from memory, but his recollection is very close to the King James Bible verses, which reads: "Now therefore kill every male among the little ones, and kill every woman that hath known man by lying with him. But all the women children, that have not known a man by lying with him, keep alive for yourselves." Interestingly, Arthur fails to mention that this was God's command, through Moses, to the Israelites after they had conquered the Midianites. Pointing this out would have strengthened his argument.

cleared up is the status of the soul as relative to the body at the time of departure. In other words, will the soul of an infant remain an infant spirit, and that of an aged person remain old? Shall we retain our identity? Will we meet and know our friends and relatives? Shall we know and see things that are transpiring on this earth? In the afterlife can we rectify mistakes made here?

FAITH

Almost all of the religious theory is hinged upon what is termed "Faith." If faith means the acceptance of any mythical concept without evidence of scientific support, like an ostrich sticking his head in the sand, then we would be much better off without it than with it. Faith has never advanced civilization. It may console, but it does not advance. It is science and invention that puts us ahead. Faith was at its highest peak during the Dark Ages and not one step forward was taken. Over a period of more than three hundred years and there was not a single invention or discovery that was not penalized with death. The Inquisition was ever alert. Then you ask, "What would we do without religion?" When one stops to consider it was necessary to separate the Church from the State in order to form a stable government, we sit up and take note. Had you noticed that the word "God" does not appear in the Constitution of the United States, nor is the Bible mentioned?

If it was necessary to drop three-fourths of the Christian religion to form a stable government and to protect science and invention, then I think we can venture a little further and drop a lot of credulities from the burdens of society. Loose the shackles of "Fear" and the thoughts of "Hell" that we may move forward in the clear atmosphere of "Nature" unabashed and unafraid. I wish to radiate life.

"Now come and let us reason together."[100] If the soul be immortal, unquenched even by death, what is its position in case of applying an anesthetic, or even a sound sleep undisturbed by a dream? Does it step aside? We observe that any tampering with the body disturbs the mind even to unconsciousness, like a stroke on the head or a rise of temperature. Is the soul likewise affected? Then, if we can nullify consciousness and resuscitate it, shall we say that chemicals are more effective than death?

If a man has an operation on the eyes and the eyes removed, and he dies twenty years later, will the eyes regain their vision? To me it is unthinkable.

Another question confronts us: What about immortality in the lower steps of animal life? Many that have bone for bone, muscle for muscle, and blood cell for blood cell. Can you assign any reason that would entitle man to the conquest over death that should be denied the lower animals? They give all they have to give, they submit to man and bear his burdens and give their life and flesh that he might live. Is there no compensation? Now, I have been talking to you from the orthodox viewpoint, but from my viewpoint the lower animal has the edge on you, for if the Scriptures be true and they have no Hell to go to, whereas you have one and not one chance in a thousand to elude it. What did Jesus tell the man that asked what should he do to inherit eternal life? As one of the requests he demanded that the man sell all of his property and give to the poor.[101] Are you going to do that? No. The way you will get out of it is by telling what Jesus meant and why, etc., etc. And it is written, "It is as impossible for a rich man to enter the Kingdom of Heaven as for a camel to

---

[100] Ironically, this quote is from Isaiah 1:18, King James Version of the Bible.
[101] This is from Matthew 19: 20, in which Jesus tells a young man, "If thou will be perfect, go and sell that thou hast, and give to the poor, and thou shalt have treasure in heaven; and come and follow me."

pass through a needle's eye."[102] Other commands are so numerous and so drastic that no human being could comply with them. Take the first of the Ten Commandments, "Thou shall love the Lord thy God with all thy mind, and thy soul, and with all thy body."[103] A fool would know this is impossible. Then to cap it off, it is said, "If you are guilty of the least of these you are guilty of the whole."[104] I had rather have no soul a thousand times than to take the chance.

WHAT OTHERS SAY

Socrates said at his execution, "If death is like a sound sleep undisturbed by even a dream, if is a wonderful gain."[105]

Henry Ward Beecher, when he came to die, said, "Now comes the mystery."[106]

Thomas Edison, when asked for his opinion of immortality, said, "Nobody knows; it makes no

---

[102] Arthur's version of this biblical quote is not quite right. In Matthew 19, 23 & 24 (King James Version), Jesus said: "Verily I say unto you, That a rich man shall hardly enter into the kingdom of Heaven. And again I say unto you, It is easier for a camel to go through the eye of a needle, than for a rich man to enter into the Kingdom of Heaven."

[103] Here, Arthur is confusing the first of the Ten Commandments with a part of the New Testament. When a lawyer asked what was necessary to do "to inherit eternal life," Jesus responded with another question, "What is written in the [Jewish] law? The man replied, "Thou shalt love the Lord thy God withal thy heart, and with all thy soul, and with all thy strength, and with all thy mind; and thy neighbor as thyself." Luke 10: 25-27 (KJV).

[104] I am not sure where Arthur got this quote. Perhaps he was thinking of Matthew 5, 19: "Whosoever therefore shall break one of these least commandments, and shall teach men so, he shall be called the least in the kingdom of heaven: but whosoever shall do and teach them, the same shall be called great in the kingdom of heaven."

[105] Once again, Arthur is close but not quite accurate. The actual quote is: "Now if there is, in fact, no awareness in death, but it is like sleep, the kind in which the sleeper does not dream at all, then death would seem to be a marvelous gain."

[106] This quote is accurate.

difference."[107]

J. Arthur Thompson said, "We have no scientific evidence of immortality."[108]

John Burroughs, when questioned, said, "I am too much interested in this good old world that still entertains me."[109]

Dr. Charles Mayo said, "I have dissected more bodies, both living and dead, possibly, than any man living today and I have found no evidence of a soul nor do I see any need for one."[110]

Rupert Hughes belongs to this category but I haven't his identical words.

Luther Burbank said, "If you will produce any reliable evidence of immortality, I will accept it, if not, not."[111]

Alex Carrrel, in his book "Man the Unknown," after repeatedly mentioning the soul, on page 118 makes clear his position, which is in part as follows: "Of course one will always speak of the soul as an entity. Just as one speaks of the setting and rising of the sun, although everyone knows since Galileo's time that the sun is relatively immobile."

---

[107] I can't find this specific quote anywhere but it *is* true that Edison was irreligious. In the *New York Times for* October 2, 1910, he said: "Nature is what we know. We do not know the gods of religions. And nature is not kind, or merciful, or loving. If God made me— the fabled God of the three qualities of which I spoke: mercy, kindness, love—He also made the fish I catch and eat. And where do His mercy, kindness, and love for that fish come in? No; nature made us —nature did it all— not the gods of the religions."

[108] I have been unable to verify this quote.

[109] Again it does not appear that Arthur got the quote quite right but it is certainly true that Burroughs was an "infidel" whose god was nature. He *did* say: "I am too much preoccupied, too much at home with myself, to feel any interest in anything that interests my fellows." Clara Barrus, *Our Friend John Burroughs* (Boston and New York: Houghton Mifflin Company, 1914), 135.

[110] I have been unable to verify this quote.

[111] I have been unable to verify this quote.

Robert Ingersoll said, "Is there life beyond the silent night another day? Is death a door that leads to light? We cannot say."[112]

If it be proper to add my concept of the philosophy of life, I would say: "Science is my God, to do good is my Religion, Oblivion is my Heaven."[113]

—The Author

Just a few more words: Were the men mentioned above meaner or more unkind or less happy than their contemporaries? I could easily double this list with names of outstanding men who have been a credit to their times. On the other hand, you would find it a task to find a moron or a criminal that is not a believer.

---

[112] This quote is accurate. Ingersoll was the nineteenth century's most celebrated American agnostic.

[113] Arthur's own philosophical stance appears to have been inspired, at least in part, by the Dutch Astronomer Christiaan Huygens and the English-American political writer Thomas Paine. Hugyens wrote: "The world is my country; to promote science is my religion." Paine wrote (in the Rights of Man): "My country is the world and my religion is to do good."

PART THREE

"A scientist's duty or purpose as you choose to call it, is to endeavor to fathom a problem as it confronts him fairly, without fear or favor and endeavor to assign causes and effects, without suggesting conditions that did not exist. We have enough at hand without building imaginary things and conditions that did not exist."

—Arthur Babb

From Camille Flammarion's *L'atmosphère: météorologie populaire* (1888).

"WHY A SCIENTIST BELIEVES IN GOD"
By A. Cressy Morrison
Reviewed by Arthur Babb

I cannot lay claim to the high honor of being a scientist as Mr. Morrison does but despite my lack of early training, I cannot help loving to browse in this old field of the gods.

Referring to Mr. Morrison's article in the *READER'S DIGEST* of Dec. '46, I wish to say I cannot go with Mr. Morrison all the way. He seems to have some preconceived idea of a god head, and sets that post as his goal, and fences the avenue with every conceivable obstacle to force the reader to his viewpoint. As to my part I approach the subject as a big question mark & pursue with what-ever evidence I can find regardless of where it may lead and can truly join hands with Thos. Huxley in saying "I will not compromise with error for mental ease."[114]

FIRST Mr. Morrison attempts to prove that the universe was designed and executed by a great intelligence. Shall we assume this intelligence to be a power outside of that of force and matter as responsible for the whole? Then the question suggests itself: where the origin and what the purpose? And we are lost in a myth the first rattle out of the box.

As to Mr. Morrison's comparison to you putting a few pennies in your pocket and then taking them out at random is ludicrous and has no part in the subject. His estimate of the earth on its axis is correct as of today but don't make the mistake of assuming it was always so, for

---

[114] Thomas H. Huxley, an English scientist and colleague of Charles Darwin, invented the term "agnostic" in 1876 as a term for someone like himself, who doubts the existence of God.

the sub-man had a much shorter day and night than we have at present and the future man will know a much longer day and night than we have as some scientists tell us that the universe is running down.

It is hard for me to accept Mr. Morrison as one of the outstanding scientists, from suggestions that he sets forth, for example: in referring to the sun and its relations to the earth, he quotes the sun's temperature at 12,000 degrees Fahrenheit; on what part of the face of the earth does that apply? He seems to assume all things fixed and himself standing at one place: How about the temperature at the poles? Is it 12,000 there? And was it always at the temperature as we know it today? Certainly not. Prehistoric man knew a hotter day than we, to say nothing of a time before the fragments that go to make up our solar system left the parent body. The sun is momently losing its radiation.

He refers to the slant of the earth at 23 degrees, which is correct, but was it always thus? And will it remain so? We cannot say. But what is the evidence? We find elephants in the Arctic region with food still in their maws, suggesting that this was once a tropical climate: What must have happened? Did the earth shift its polarity so quickly that the beasts did not have time for migration? And we have no assurance that it will not repeat this feat.

He next comments on the moon and explains what would happen ("if") it was 50,000 miles away: the effect on the tides, etc. He repeatedly injects those (ifs). As I understand the subject, (if) is superfluous in dealing with nature. It suggests a change in conditions that didn't exist.

A scientist's duty or purpose as you choose to call it, is to endeavor to fathom a problem as it confronts him fairly, without fear or favor and endeavor to assign causes and effects, without suggesting conditions that did not exist. We have enough at hand without building imaginary things and conditions that did not exist.

SECOND: In this preamble Mr. Morrison comments on the resourcefulness of life to accomplish its purpose, but he fails to explain what that purpose might be. He exhausts himself in trying to mystify the subject as much as possible he then asserts that "Nature did not create life." Here we disagree. I say that Force and Matter is responsible for all forms of life that we now see: there is no other source. Mr. Morrison winds up with a question "Who then has put it here? This would not have been a surprise to me coming from the man in the street, but as coming from a scientist, it was little less than a shock.

There lurks in the human mind a lure for mystery or myth, which has its origin at the root of superstition. This mystifying trend of mind is not prevalent among scientists, though they are not wholly immune, Whitehead and Morrison are strongly tainted, but Julian Huxley, Jas. Jeans and Shapley, and a number of others are fairly free so far as I can tell.

Articles put out by those near-scientists have an ill affect upon the average mind struggling under the load of superstition.

THIRD: In this section Mr. Morrison's comments on animal and fish life, their behavior, etc., is interesting and makes good reading; though nothing new, this was all known to piscatorians and fishermen centuries ago, but remarkable to say the least. But if I was calling upon to assign reasons, I would say "All life behaves as designed by the forces of nature and could not have done otherwise."

FOURTH: In this section the author deals with man and I was glad to note his reference to the faculty of "Reason." This is the Algebra of human thought, that element of mind that takes up where the five senses leave off, enabling man to solve problems that lie beyond the realms of the five senses. It is such a pity that this power of thought has been so dwarfed and hamstringed by tradition and superstition.

I can nearly agree with Mr. Morrison on this entire section.

FIFTH: I check Mr. Morrison on this entire section except his last paragraph , in this I reserve my right to say I don't know and grant him his to think he does.

SIXTH: I can't go all the way with Bro. Morrison in this chapter, that faculty of reason that he praised so much in the fourth chapter revolts. For example he says "By the economy of nature, we are forced to realize that only infinite wisdom could have foreseen and prepared with such astute husbandry." Straightaway he sets forth an example that neither exhibits economy nor foresight: that in the case of the cactus and the insects. Assuming to be the creator with foresight, the case would be comparable to a farmer that would open a gap in his fence and turn a drove of hogs into his corn field, and after they had done much damage, he goes and gets the dogs and turns them in upon the hogs. Would be either wisdom or economy? Certainly not, we would be justified in calling him a foolish farmer.

Assuming this infinity referred to be a God that made a cactus to do much harm, then insects to destroy the cactus, instead of making neither, we would justly say it was an act of a foolish god and unjust to the people.

SEVENTH: I regret that even to the last chapter, I am forced to take issue with the author, who says "The fact that man can conceive the idea of God is in itself a unique proof." I would ask "What man and what god? Egypt had over three thousand gods." It seems that Mr. Morrison considers the world only from one place and that where he stands: and the concept of man only from his viewpoint. He asserts that "The conception of God rises from a divine faculty of man." Not as I see it. The concept and creation of gods had its origin in fear! Primitive man in his fright of the upheavals of nature, such lightning and thunder, earthquakes and volcanos created himself gods and attempted to appease the wrath of these gods to escape the rage of the elements: all manner of beast, reptile and fowls have been worshiped, the druids worshiped trees. Man was the last thing to be deified and "Man made God in his own image." Plato said "If a camel should make himself a god, it would doubtless have four feet and a hump on its back."

But that dominating "Fear" that inspired the concept of a god for primitive man, still holds good and is the dominate power behind the God of modern man.

(But who will admit it?)

Photo courtesy Library of Congress, Washington, D.C.

GOD IN THE PRIZE RING
(From *This and That*)

Editor's Note: *This story, which was inspired by an article in a local newspaper, is a wonderful example of Arthur's delightful tongue-in-cheek way of poking fun at believers. At the same time it asks a question that is still being debated today: Do people really think God would take sides in a sporting event?*

July 23, 1927

I see in this morning's paper, an article by the beautiful Estelle Taylor Dempsey, wife of the notorious Jack, and in explaining why the ex-champion won over his young opponent, the movie star admits conspiracy. She says, "I asked God to let Jack win."[115]

Suppose that we should find out that an umpire had caused a pugilist to win a fight by reason of requests of his fair spouse. He would have to fell to jail for safety.

Next comes the question: Did Sharkey's wife sleep on her rights by not interceding for her young husband? Or did she have too much respect for God to ask him to step down off his throne into the prize ring for her selfish desire?

But I wonder how the man felt that had his money up on Sharkey when he read the actress' confession. He must have felt like he had been buncoed.[116]

But this is not the first time that we have had an inkling that God was taking part in sport. We all can remember when Gene Tunney snatched the crown from this same old ex-champion. After the fight, the priest who had baptized Gene years before said enough to make us suspicious that it was God that put pep in the young

---

[115] Arthur must have read this in the *Dallas Journal* or *Dallas Times Herald*. I have been unable to find it in the *Dallas Morning News* historical archive. I *have* found it however, in papers published in other cities, so it *is* true that Mrs. Dempsey said this.
[116] Cheated or swindled.

75

pugilist's punch that made Jack wobble in almost every round.

Now, looking forward to the coming fight in September; when Jack is to meet Gene [Tunney] the second time, a most confusing problem confronts us. Suppose that the fair actress again beseeches God to make her "Lord Victorious" and the Priest that baptized Gene puts in a plea for his ward, what will happen?

("Who knows, I wonder.")

Shall I be carried to the skies on flowery beds of ease,
Whilst others fought to win the prize and sailed through bloody seas?"[117]

GOD GOES BACK ON JACK

Now that the fistolistic[118] contest between Gene Tunney and Jack Dempsey is over, and Gene beat Jack to a cold finish, what shall we say? Did the movie star lay down on her job and fail to perform her part as well in this act as in the one before when Jack sent Sharkey down for the count in the 7th round, with the assistance of God at the request of the movie actress? Or did some more influential friend take the matter up and make it plain to God that it was to the interest of humanity that Gene wore the dog collar a while longer? Or did Gene take it upon himself to do the job on his own accord?

"Who knows, I wonder."

"Oh Lord! Have we not in thy name
Cast out devils, and in thy name
Done many wonderful works?"[119]

---

[117] This is from a hymn titled "Am I a Soldier of the Cross?" Again, Arthur has some of the words wrong but it's nearly correct.
[118] This is clearly Arthur's own made-up word and I like it!
[119] This seems to be Arthur's version of Matthew 7:22.

A CRIMINAL AND HIS VICTIM, OR THE HIGHER COURT
(From *This and That*)

Editor's note: *On January 14, 1921, six bandits held up the downtown Dallas post office, making off with $46,000 in cash and $200,000 in Liberty Bonds. During the robbery, two post office clerks were shot and wounded. One of the robbers was killed in an automobile accident while trying to get away. All the others were apprehended.[120] After one of the post office clerks, George W. Street, died from his wounds on January 26, 1921, Albert Rowan—the so-called "mastermind" of the robbery and scion of a prominent Dallas family— was charged by the State of Texas with murder. In 1921 he was convicted and sentenced to a fifty-year term in prison.[121] The following year Rowan was brought to trial in federal court for the post office robbery. Following conviction, he was sentenced to twenty-five years in the federal penitentiary at Leavenworth, Kansas.[122]*

In 1926, after several prominent citizens, including Bishop James Lynch of the Dallas diocese and Reverend P. J. Lynch, attested to Rowan's good character prior to the robbery, Governor Miriam A. "Ma" Ferguson, granted Rowan a pardon on the murder conviction by the State of Texas. It does not appear, however, that he was released on parole from Leavenworth until much later.

In the imagined scenario that follows, Mrs. Street and her daughter, who have died and gone to Heaven, encounter Rowan after he too has died after becoming a "born again" Christian. Unfortunately, in this invented chance meeting, murder victim G. W. Street has gone to Hell, because although he was a good man, he never professed his faith in Jesus nor was he ever baptized. Street's wife and especially his daughter are dismayed by the apparent moral defect of this situation, whereby the forgiven murder enjoys eternal bliss while his victim, despite being a good person, must suffer the burning pit of Hell for all eternity.

---

[120] *Dallas Morning News*, January 16, 1921.
[121] *Dallas Morning News*, January 29 & May 21, 1921.
[122] *Dallas Morning News*, November 19, 1922.

Clearly, the purpose of this essay is to point out that the obvious injustice of such a situation is inconsistent with the Christian view of God and Jesus as being fair and merciful, therefore calling into question the veracity of Christian teachings.

A few days ago I noticed an item in our daily paper, that the Governor, M. A. Ferguson, had granted a full and unconditional pardon to Albert Rowan; the mastermind that instigated the Jackson St. Post office robbery of Dallas in 1923,[123] in which a postal clerk by the name of Street lost his life.

It will be remembered that Rowan was tried here in the State's court and assessed a penalty of 50 years in the penitentiary for his share in the crime. He was again tried in the Federal Court, and drew a sentence of 25 years in the Leavenworth prison.

Mr. Street left a widow and three children to mourn his loss. Mr. Rowan left a wife and an aged father and mother.

Now that the Governor has forgiven Mr. Rowan for his share in the murder of Mr. Street, and for which he has not served a day, and in as much that he was eligible for a pardon by the federal authorities after serving one fourth of his term; we have reason to expect him back among us restored to full citizenship in about two years.

But how about the widow and orphans? What has the Governor done to relieve the life of sorrow and suffering inflicted upon them by Mr. Rowan's fiendish act? Did she so much as send them a word of condolence? Or a wreath of flowers to lay upon the grave of the husband and father on the anniversary of his death? I dare say she did not so much as give them a thought.

Of all the pardons granted by the Governor, some for the most atrocious crimes in the annals of history, not

---

[123] Arthur was mistaken. The robbery occurred in 1921.

in a single instance do we see where she has sympathized with the victim, or considered the affect upon society.

JUSTICE IN ANOTHER LIFE

In face of facts set forth, we bow our heads in sorrow and hope for justice in a higher court, for it is written "Verily I say unto you, he will avenge you speedily."

Therefore let us draw an imaginary picture based on Scriptural tradition and our religious faith and see what we have a right to expect.

Let us begin by supposing that Mr. Rowan returns and takes up life among us fully restored to citizenship. He considers his mistakes and endeavors to profit by them, by obeying the laws of the State, as well as that of Society. Yea he goes further. He petitions the church, repents, believes and is baptized.

In the meantime Mrs. Street under the weight of sorrow and ill health succumbs and is laid to rest beside the remains of the husband and father. She was indeed a good and thoughtful woman and had done the thing that the husband had neglected; she had joined the church and was baptized.

A year later Mr. Rowan lost his life in an automobile accident and took his place in the same cemetery and the same minister had preached the funerals of both and in each case he assured us that the departed had gone where there was no "sorrow, sickness or death." And if our traditional opinion be true he was right, for is it not written that "whomsoever that believeth in me and is baptized, shall not perish but have everlasting life?"

One of Mrs. Street's little girls had followed her shortly after her death, and taken up her abode with the Mother.

THE MEETING

When Mr. Rowan arrived at the celestial gate he needed no passport; the Governor of the state had pardoned him, the church had accepted him in its fold, and as Jesus had forgiven the thief on the cross, even so had he forgiven Mr. Rowan. And St. Peter had been advised to that effect. So the gate swung wide and St. Peter stepped back and bowed low and bade Mr. Rowan pass thru and partake of all the pleasures that Heaven had to offer the faithful.

Mr. Rowan had not completed his first tour of the city before meeting Mrs. Street and the little daughter! Their first meeting since in the court room at that awful trial. How different the circumstances. They recognized each other. Mrs. Street shrank back and almost turned in her tracks at the sight of her husband's slayer. But then remembered that they were in heaven where there should be no horror or fear or malice. Mr. Rowan smiled and extended his hand. They were standing at the entrance of a beautiful park, at the back of which was a great precipice. They turned and walked slowly, the little girl followed in amazement and occasionally jerking at her mother's angelic robe to attract attention. Finally, in a lull of conversation, she exclaimed, "Mama! Mama! Who is this man"? "Why this is Mr. Rowan daughter." The child remembered the name. "Oh Mama is this that horrid man that killed Papa when the post office was robbed and left us alone in the other world?" "Hush!" exclaimed the mother, "Hush my child, you must not think of any one as horrid. This is heaven, and there are no horrid people here. You don't understand; the governor has pardoned him in the other world and Jesus has forgiven him, so we must forgive him too." "But Mama what crime did Papa commit that the governor and Jesus would not forgive him? He did not kill someone or rob people. You have told me that we had a good daddy." She could see that the father was missing and doubtless knew something of his miserable plight. Mr. Rowan had stood listening to the child's inquiry, and added she doesn't understand. And indeed, she did not. Then the mother attempted to explain by saying, "Listen my child, your father did not kill anyone or did he rob, and indeed he was a good man, but he did not belong to any church, nor had he been baptized and am not sure that he even believed the 'Holy Bible' to be the word of God."

They turned and walked to the back of the park as though impelled by some magic force and stood at that great precipice, upon the very spot where Lazarus stood when he viewed Dives in Hell,[124] they likewise could see the father wrapped in those torturous flames. He looked up into the face of his wife and child and cried aloud, entreating them to intercede for his relief, saying, "I beseech thee to appear before St. Peter and implore him to offer a petition for me, and if he will not hear, appeal to the throne of the most high; ask Jesus to intercede for me. Tell them that I have obeyed the laws of my country, and have administered to the poor and afflicted of yonder land, and that I have been a good and kind husband and father and that my life was taken while at my duty, and with no time for thought or reflection."

She appeared before St. Peter and delivered the message, to which he replied, "Those things are the affairs of the other world over which I have no control, see thou to that. She then appeared before the throne of the most high and delivered her appeal, to which Jesus replied in a kind but firm tone, "Had he not the book? Did I not when I was yet on earth say that unless ye accept and be born again, ye cannot enter the kingdom of heaven? She turned and walked away; not sorrowful, for there can be no sorrow in heaven, but reconciled to the inevitable. So must it be.

She returned to the park where Mr. Rowan and the little girl were waiting. They walked across the park to be

---

[124] See New Testament Bible, Luke 16:19-13.

seated far enough from the pit to not be disturbed by the moans of the wicked. Mr. Rowan broke the silence by saying "My good lady I am a most fortunate as well as a most happy man; and I owe my good fortune to so many things, that I do not know to which I am the most indebted. Perhaps if there was a scale by which we could measure such things, I would owe the greatest share to your unfortunate husband." "No," she interrupted, "to the mercy of Jesus" "I knew you would say that," he replied, "but you are not a good philosopher. You see one must first have something to bring him to Jesus. The fact is my salvation had its origin in crime in which your poor husband was a victim. That seems strange at first thought, but let me explain. If left to the ordinary trend of my life, I doubtless would have drifted along as most men do up to the time of the accident that ended my life, and died without repentance, and would have shared the fate of your poor husband. But having been convicted and while serving my sentence I considered my error and repented of my sins. Jesus forgave my sins and Mrs. Ferguson pardoned my crime; we belong to the same church. How small were those bags of money, even though I had succeeded in escaping with them as compared to my happy State! How little did I know that I was 'laying up treasures that moths cannot corrupt or thieves break through and steal.'"

"Well," she exclaimed, "It seems that it has thus turned out that the good man has landed in Hell while the criminal is elevated a heavenly estate." "But you see," he said, "the works of God are mysterious and we must not question." "But," she added, "Have you considered your victim? Do you realize that your influence has permeated your associates in the other world, and is still bearing fruit? And that your crimes are still wielding their weight of sorrow upon those that yet remain?" "You must not question affairs of this nature; he doeth all things well." They arose and walked again to the precipice at the rear of the park to the place where Lazarus stood and the victim of a dastardly crime saw the instigator enjoying the association of his wife and child, while he writhed in the flames of Hell.

Jan. 1927

Sure enough, the papers have just announced that Mr. Rowan together with Dr. Frederick Cook, who has also been serving a term at Leavenworth, will soon be at liberty, and Dallas' wave of crime will be capped with the trophy of their presence in the near future! The statement said they would engage in the "cold storage" business.[125]

Now if you have any "diabolical plots and schemes" that you don't want to taint before you can cook the public; put them in storage with "Cook and Rowan." They will guarantee to keep them cold and confidential, if the cook has to go to the North Pole to get the ice.

---

[125] I am not sure in which newspaper Arthur saw this reported. The earliest reference for Cook that I have been able to find in 1927 is in the *Dallas Morning News*, March 3, 1927, but there is no mention of Rowan. However, the *Dallas Morning News*, March 11, 1930 confirms that Cook planned to go into the cold storage business with Rowan, who had been "recommended for parole and is expected to leave the penitentiary within a few days."

SCHEDULED FOR PUBLICATION IN 2016

By

THE FREETHOUGHT PRESS OF TEXAS

GUIDED BY REASON:
THE GOLDEN AGE OF FREETHOUGHT IN TEXAS

By Steven R. Butler and Others

THE TEXAS FREETHOUGHT READER
A Companion to GUIDED BY REASON

Edited By
Steven R. Butler